AUTHOR'S PREFACE

When we speak of popularity in terms of snakes in the hobby of herpetology, it is inevitable that the genus *Lampropeltis* will come up in the conversation at one point or another. The snakes of this genus are known in vernacular terms as the kingsnakes and the Milk Snakes, and anyone heavily involved in this wonderful hobby knows them well. In the book you are holding now, we will be discussing the former of the two, the Milk Snakes, because they are *so* popular that an entire book focused on them exclusively could very easily "hold water," as the saying goes.

The Milk Snakes are, after all, wonderful creatures. There are so many beautiful subspecies to study, and their life histories are so fascinating, that it would take years to really get a firm grip on the subject in its entirety. And it really is no surprise that the hobbyists, myself included, are so mad about them. They are not only striking in pattern in color, they are also voracious eaters, willing breeders, and never grow to a size so large that they could be termed "unmanageable."

So, with all this love and lust going on, there is of course a need for pertinent literature as well; hence the reason for a book of this nature. You don't have to slog through a swamp of irrelevant paragraphs to find every tiny tidbit of information concerning the snakes you're keeping—this book is designed specifically for the Milk Snakes and the Milk Snakes only. I, the author, have kept and bred a number of Milk Snake varieties and have gathered literature and spoken to professional keepers concerning many more. There's a little something in here for everyone: taxonomy, natural history, breeding info, diseases, etc. It is a complete work, and most importantly, a practical, useful one.

It is my sincere wish that it serves you well.

W. P. Mara

Lampropeltis triangulum campbelli (Pueblan Milk Snake). The Pueblan Milk Snake is one of a handful of Milk Snake varieties currently being bred in captivity on a regular basis.

W. P. MARA

This book is dedicated to the memory of Dr. Clarence John "Jack" McCoy 25 July 1935 to 7 July 1993 Whose contributions to herpetology can never be measured, and whose contributions to friendship will always be missed.

While there are many snakes that have, at best, only vague bits of information concerning their background, the Milk Snakes have been much-studied throughout the decades and thus a deluge of highly detailed data is available concerning them.

TAXONOMY

The nomenclatural history of the Milk Snakes is both fascinating and somewhat confusing. There have been feel the Milk Snake's first naming began with Lacepede in 1788 with *Coluber triangulum*. It should be mentioned however that a third name, *Coluber eximius*, was used by Harlan in 1827 to describe a specimen that was supposedly from the Pennsylvania area. Although the truth of the matter seems to be unclear at present, the late Dr. C. J. McCoy of the Carnegie Museum proposed in 1972 that the latter name be considered a valid Milk Snake synonym nevertheless.

Lampropeltis triangulum gaigae (Black Milk Snake).

W.P. MARA

so many changes in the Latin classification of this species since it was first described in 1766 that the list of synonyms alone could fill up this page.

In the first place, the original description of *Coluber doliatus*, being made by Karl von Linne (Carolus Linneaus) in 1766, may not have even concerned a Milk Snake, but instead a Scarlet Snake, now known as *Cemophora coccinea*. This mystery has been the subject of much debate throughout the years and remains unsolved.

Thus, most taxonomic historians

There are a large number of other names attached to the many Milk Snake subspecies as well, but these are so plentiful that it would be a waste of both time and paper to go into it here. We are primarily concerned with only the earliest origins of the Milk Snake taxonomy and its status today. For a more detailed discussion of this engrossing topic, refer to Kenneth L. Williams's work, *Systematics and Natural History of the American Milk Snake, Lampropeltis triangulum* (1988, Milwaukee Public Museum).

The genus for the Milk Snakes as we know it today, *Lampropeltis*, first came to light in 1853 when it was described by Fitzinger, but it really didn't start being applied to the Milk Snakes until the early 1900's when Stejneger described *Lampropeltis pyrrhomelaena celaenops* in 1903, then he and Barbour recognized both *L. elapsoides* and *L. triangulum* in their *North American Checklist of Amphibians and Reptiles* (1917). Finally in 1920, Blanchard published a monograph on *Lampropeltis* covering *L. elapsoides virginianum, L. triangulum nelsoni,* and *L. ruthveni* (this last one being named after noted herpetologist Alexander Ruthven and is, most interestingly, now no longer considered a Milk Snake). The word *Lampropeltis* itself comes from two Greek derivatives— *lampros,* meaning shiny, and *peltis,* which means shield. *Triangulum* means triangle.

There are presently 25 recognized subspecies of the Milk Snakes, although it should be pointed out that the concept of subspecies in the first place is considered by many workers to be bogus and unworthy of respect or recognition. It seems that such classifications rest on soft, unstable bases and are thus subject to frequent change. It is not at all my intent to "shake up" any foundations or express personal views, but it is important that the interested reader be made aware of the "flimsiness," if you will, of such a category. Many students begin their education in systematics under the impression that nomenclature is a permanent structure built on rock-solid reasoning; I assure you that most classifications undoubtedly are not.

GEOGRAPHY

The Milk Snake is unquestionably what one would call a strong "survivor" species, and one of the most common characteristics of such groups is something called widespread distribution. In simple terms, this means the Milk Snakes as a whole cover a large area.

In the north, *Lampropeltis triangulum* can be found in both southern Quebec and southern Ontario. This is truly remarkable for any reptile since they are not usually known for their tolerance to colder environments.

In the west, *triangulum* goes as far as the Rockies, but not beyond. This means quite simply that there are no Milk Snakes on the West Coast of North America. On the East Coast, however, it is a different story; Milk Snakes cover that part of the continent from Maine to Florida.

South is perhaps the area where the

Lampropeltis triangulum amaura (Louisiana Milk Snake) The Milk Snakes received their name from the bizarre belief that they sucked milk from cows. This, of course, is untrue.

W. P. MARA

Milk Snakes leave their most indelible geographical imprint. Subspecies are known from Mexico, Colombia, Ecuador, and the Cordillera de la

Costa de Venezuela. This last locale is one place where the attractive Ecuadorian Milk Snake, *Lampropeltis triangulum micropholis*, occurs.

HABITAT

Since the Milk Snake is such a wide-ranging creature, it occurs in quite a variety of natural habitats. Milk Snakes have been found in wooded stream valleys, open prairies, on the edges of cultivated fields, in sandy pine forests, rocky canyons, mountain slopes, pine-oak forests, small grassy patches near human development, and even in close proximity to salt water. The key of course is to know which subspecies you're dealing with and go from there, but the obvious bottom line is that there is no single natural area in which the Milk Snake thrives; there are many.

GENERAL IDENTIFICATION

As with all creatures, Milk Snakes can be diagnosed by a number of morphological

infralabials 9 (8 to 10). Postoculars 2, preoculars 1, and loreals, most interestingly, number 1 except in some specimens from the southeastern United States, where they may be absent entirely. The head is generally not very pronounced from the rest of the body and is more rounded than square (as in many *Elaphe*, for example). Ventrals run from 154 to 236 (males) and 161 to 244 (females), and subcaudals from 32 to 63 (males) and 31 to 60 (females). The maxillary (upper jaw) teeth number from 11 to 15, and the posterior two on each side will be slightly larger than those preceding them (an obscure but technically useful characteristic of the Milk Snakes). Basic ground color is red (or orangish red, brown, and sometimes gray), with black and yellow or white rings or saddles. The belly can be either very whitish (almost uniformly so) or have a checked pattern consisting of a dullish

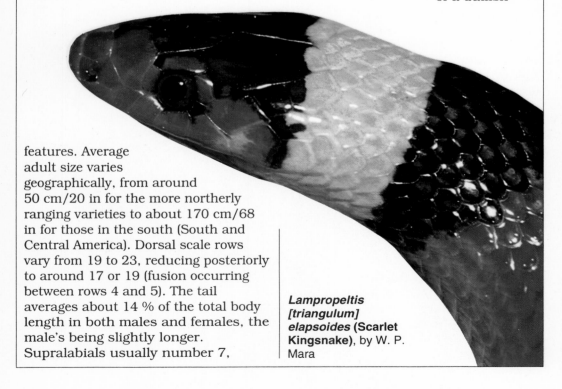

features. Average adult size varies geographically, from around 50 cm/20 in for the more northerly ranging varieties to about 170 cm/68 in for those in the south (South and Central America). Dorsal scale rows vary from 19 to 23, reducing posteriorly to around 17 or 19 (fusion occurring between rows 4 and 5). The tail averages about 14 % of the total body length in both males and females, the male's being slightly longer. Supralabials usually number 7,

Lampropeltis [triangulum] elapsoides (Scarlet Kingsnake), by W. P. Mara

SCOTT BALLARD

Lampropeltis triangulum abnorma
(Guatemalan Milk Snake).

bone-white with either simple black
checks or black with reddish orange;
the dorsal bands usually do not
number over 30 in any variety.

THE SUBSPECIES

As it was pointed out earlier, there
are currently 25 accepted Milk
Snakes subspecies. For the purpose
of completeness, each one is
mentioned here followed by a brief
discussion. To give credit where it
is due, much of this information has
simply been gleaned from Ronnie
Markel's excellent TFH book,
Kingsnakes and Milk Snakes (1989),
and from Ken Williams' equally
fascinating systematic Milk Snake
book mentioned earlier.

Guatemalan Milk Snake
Lampropeltis triangulum abnorma
(Bocourt, 1866)
Ranging from northeastern Chipas,
Mexico southward into northwestern
Guatemala and Honduras, this snake
can be found in a wide variety of
habitats. It is not not often seen in
the pet trade, but reportedly will take
lizards and occasionally small mice.
The young are notably prettier than
the adults. One of the most
distinguishing features is the broad
white band on the snout while the

rest of the head is a glossy black.
Louisiana Milk Snake
Lampropeltis triangulum amaura
(Cope, 1861)
Not a very large snake, *L. t. amaura*
rarely reaches beyond two and a half
feet. It can be easily distinguished by
the mostly red snout which is
occasionally flecked with black and/or
white. It is one of the Milk Snakes
often seen in the hobby (although not
one of the *most* popular) and can
command a high price. It ranges from
southern Arkansas and Oklahoma to
Louisiana and the Gulf Coast of Texas.
Andean Milk Snake
Lampropeltis triangulum andesiana
Williams, 1978
One of the most recently described
subspecies, this Milk Snake got its

W. W. LAMAR

Lampropeltis triangulum amaura

vernacular (common) name from its
exclusive locality—the Andes
Mountains in Colombia. The base color
is, unsurprisingly, red, with a series of
pairs of thin black bands interspaced
with a thin white band, and adults
have a medium black overall tint that
makes them appear somewhat dull.
They are virtually never seen in the
hobby.
Mexican Milk Snake
Lampropeltis triangulum annulata

southern Texas and runs south from there into Tamaulipas, Mexico.

Jalisco Milk Snake

Lampropeltis triangulum arcifera (Werner, 1903)

A snake largely resembling the aforementioned *L. t. annulata*, the great difference between them being *arcifera*'s mostly red belly. The number of dorsal red rings on this snake varies enormously—anywhere from 14 to 31—which also makes accurate identification rather difficult. It ranges basically in southwestern Mexico, gaining its name from a state known as Jalisco, where it occurs around Lake Chapala. Like many of the other Milk Snake varieties, this one is almost never seen in the herp hobby.

Blanchard's Milk Snake

DR. R. S. FUNK.

Lampropeltis triangulum arcifera (Jalisco Milk Snake).

Lampropeltis triangulum blanchardi Stuart, 1935

A native of the Yucatan Peninsula, this interesting Milk Snake intergrades with the Guatemalan Milk Snake, *L. t. abnorma* in the extreme southern part of its range. It can be distinguished fairly easily by the complete black ring at the start of the dorsum, and beyond

W. W. LAMAR

Lampropeltis triangulum andesiana (Andean Milk Snake).

(Kennicott, 1861)

The word "annulata" literally means "ringed," and rightly so in the case of this particular snake; *L. t. annulata*'s yellow bands run right across the belly, making it a truly ringed snake. It also has a black head and snout (the latter sometimes being invaded by vague white mottling), but the red and yellow scales are pure rather than tipped with black or brown, as in the case with many other Milk Snakes. Its range begins in

Lampropeltis triangulum annulata (Mexican Milk Snake).

R. G. MARKEL

that some of the other black rings touch along the center of the dorsum. This is a lowland and deciduous forest dweller that spends most of its active time during the night. It is rare.

Pueblan Milk Snake

Lampropeltis triangulum campbelli Quinn, 1983

Although considered one of the "newer" Milk Snakes, the Pueblan has enjoyed an impressive degree of commercial popularity. It has a distinctly mottled snout (white on

Lampropeltis triangulum blanchardi
(Blanchard's Milk Snake).

D. P. MUTH

JOHN R. QUINN

Lampropeltis triangulum celaenops

black, with the white forming a vague horseshoe shape) and broad, radiant white rings which slightly resemble those on the newborns of other Milk Snake species. Occurring from southern Puebla into northern Oaxaca, Mexico, it was named after Jonathan A. Campbell.

New Mexico Milk Snake

Lampropeltis triangulum celaenops

Stejneger, 1903

This attractive little Milk Snake rarely reaches over two feet. It occurs in oak forests, pinyon juniper woodlands, and gamma grass areas, and feeds mainly on lizards. It can be found only in the Rio Grande drainage region of eastern New Mexico and

southwestern Texas. It has broad orange bands flanked by considerably smaller white ones, and the black bands begin to curve toward each

W. B. ALLEN, JR.

Lampropeltis triangulum campbelli
(Pueblan Milk Snake).

Lampropeltis triangulum annulata (Mexican Milk Snake), by B. Kahl.

other on the dorsum, but never actually touch. *Celaenops* is only occasionally seen in the hobby.

Conant's Milk Snake

Lampropeltis triangulum conanti
Williams, 1978

Named after the accomplished herpetologist Dr. Roger Conant, this snake has, as far as I know, never been seen in the herpetological hobby. Its dorsal pattern is quite distinct in having only small black rings, and very often those are reduced to only small round saddles with centers of hazy orange. These markings are well apart from each other. There is also a tendency for the black area on the posterior portion of the head to run, at the median, into the first black ring

Lampropeltis triangulum dixoni (Dixon's Milk Snake).

bands of a very pale yellow. The head and snout are black, but the nape is also a pale yellow, then solid black again before the red on the dorsum begins. Dixon's Milk Snake was named after J. R. Dixon, who wrote, among other things, a taxonomic synopsis of the amphibians and reptiles of Texas in 1987. Although the description of this snake was not recorded until 1983, the holotype, a female, was collected on July 27, 1969 and placed in the Texas Cooperative Wildlife Collection.

Scarlet Kingsnake

Lampropeltis elapsoides
(considered by many to still be
Lampropeltis triangulum elapsoides)
(Holbrook, 1838)

Perhaps the most celebrated and well-known of all the Milk Snakes, it not only bears the confusing vernacular name "kingsnake," but more than a few professionals believe this animal to be its own species

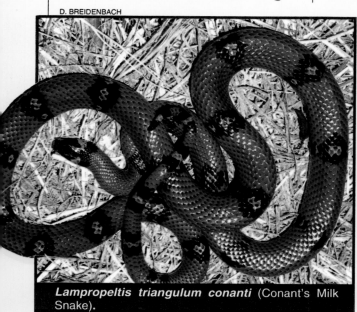

Lampropeltis triangulum conanti (Conant's Milk Snake).

and/or saddle. This snake occurs mainly in the Sierre Madre del Sur and parts of Oaxaca, Mexico.

Dixon's Milk Snake

Lampropeltis triangulum dixoni
Quinn, 1983

The black rings on this snake are very broad, almost eclipsing the red in some places. Between them are thin

altogether! It can be easily recognized by its totally red snout and small, slender body (rarely over 20 inches), and is a difficult, if not unwilling, captive. Every now and then a keeper will get lucky and come across a specimen that eats pinkie mice, but the primary food is small lizards and sometimes small snakes—difficult

R. G. MARKEL

Lampropeltis [triangulum] elapsoides
(Scarlet Kingsnake).

Pine Snake, *Pituophis melanoleucus lodingi*, the Black Milk Snake starts life with much the same appearance as the others of its species—patterned and colored. But as it grows, the colors slowly become suppressed by a very dark tint until eventually the animal is completely black (sometimes with a bit of gold between the scales). It occurs in the mountains of Costa Rica and Panama and is occasionally seen in the hobby.

Central Plains Milk Snake
Lampropeltis triangulum gentilis
(Baird and Girard, 1853)

PAUL FREED

Lampropeltis triangulum gaigae (Black Milk Snake).

items for virtually anyone to supply. They are also known for a remarkable lack of calm and will thrash about in one's hand until returned to their tank. Nevertheless, they are enormously popular in the hobby and have been captive-bred for many years.

Black Milk Snake
Lampropeltis triangulum gaigae
Dunn 1937

A most remarkable snake, it is considered by many to represent a purely melanistic race of Milk Snakes. Similar to the Black

DR. R. S. FUNK.

Lampropeltis triangulum gaigae (Black Milk Snake).

If any Milk Snake could be called a "cult favorite," it's this one. While most hobbyists and pet stores are hardly even aware of the Central Plains Milk Snake's existence, there is a small fraternity of others who have been buying and breeding them for years. They are most attractive, having somewhere around 30 brilliant·black and red to orange rings on the dorsum

R. G. MARKEL

Lampropeltis triangulum gentilis (Central Plains Milk Snake).

hobbyists are concerned—normal phase, and the popular "tangerine" phase (hence its sometimes being called the Tangerine Milk Snake). It is one of the larger Milk Snakes, reaching about four feet in length, and occurs in parts of Honduras, Nicaragua, and eastern Costa Rica. This is a creature of low to medium elevation. It can be sustained on mice and lizards in captivity and is not difficult to breed.

Ecuadorian Milk Snake
Lampropeltis triangulum micropholis
(Cope, 1861)

lying over a beautiful wheat-tan color. They are known for an even temperament and a remarkable adaptability to captivity, and will take mice without fuss.

Honduran Milk Snake
Lampropeltis triangulum hondurensis
Williams, 1978
Another hobby favorite, the Honduran Milk Snake was described only in 1978. It occurs in two main color "varieties," at least as far as

SCOTT BALLARD

Lampropeltis triangulum micropholis (Ecuadorian Milk Snake).

Lampropeltis triangulum hondurensis (Honduran Milk Snake).

The largest of the Milk Snakes, some specimens have been known to reach a length of over five and a half feet. It is also, most interestingly, the most southerly ranging Milk Snake as well, occurring in the Canal Zone, eastern Panama, and parts of south and central Ecuador. It can be distinguished by a short series of 10 to 18 broad dorsal rings and a grouping of yellow scales on the head that are pure in color rather than tainted or outlined in black. This snake is virtually never offered to hobbyists.

DR. R. S. FUNK

D. BREIDENBACH

Lampropeltis triangulum multistrata (Pale Milk Snake).

multistrata is most distinctive in that it is a blatant pale orange color flecked with black. The Pale Milk Snake is known to intergrade with both *L. t. gentilis* and *L. t. syspila.*

Nelson's Milk Snake
Lampropeltis triangulum nelsoni
Blanchard, 1920

There is very little known about the life history of this animal. Not only is its natural range scattered and erratic, but it also intergrades heavily with a number of other subspecies. Furthermore, the majority of its natural habitat,

Pale Milk Snake
Lampropeltis triangulum multistrata
(Kennicott, 1861)

The word "multistrata" means "much-covered" or "many-layered" although what it precisely refers to on this snake is unknown. It is a handsome animal with a whitish ground color complemented by rich red saddles that are often broken at the top by the touching of the black rings that flank them. The snout of

W. W. LAMAR

Lampropeltis triangulum oligozona (Pacific American Milk Snake).

Lampropeltis triangulum nelsoni (Nelson's Milk Snake).

D. SODERBERG

consisting mainly of tropical forest, is difficult for herpetologists to work in. It is a remarkably striking snake, bearing more than a passing resemblance to the immensely popular Sinaloan Milk Snake, *Lampropeltis triangulum sinaloae*, the main difference being that the red rings are only about twice the length of the black and whites, whereas in *sinaloae* they are about three times as wide.

Pacific American Milk Snake
Lampropeltis triangulum oligozona
(Bocourt, 1886)

A somewhat rare snake, the status of the Pacific American Milk Snake as a valid subspecies has been questioned. Not only is its range fairly difficult to define, but many specimens show distinct morphological influence from other nearby subspecies. The supposed range is described as "the Pacific slope from the village of Tehuantepec in Oaxaca, east and south along the coast and adjacent foothills of Chipas, Mexico, and Guatemala." Even upon close examination this snake looks much like all the others in the Mexican and Central American vicinity.

Lampropeltis triangulum sinaloae (Sinaloan Milk Snake).

Lampropeltis triangulum polyzona (Atlantic Central American Milk Snake).

Atlantic Central American Milk Snake

Lampropeltis triangulum polyzona (Cope, 1861)

A fairly easy snake to distinguish, looking at the head one sees that the scales around the nostrils are distinctively white while the remainder of the snout is black. The remainder of the dorsum consists of the normal red/black/white/black/red arrangement, the red rarely, if ever, being invaded by the black rings. This is a snake of tropical rainforests and has occasionally been found in high elevation regions. It too intergrades with other subspecies and is rarely seen in the herp hobby.

Sinaloan Milk Snake

Lampropeltis triangulum sinaloae Williams, 1978

Perhaps the most successful "new kid on the block" in the snake-keeping hobby, the Sinaloan Milk Snake deserves its fame—it is one of the most striking serpents in the world. While it does bear the standard Milk Snake red/black/white pattern, the red is a deep, rich, almost radiant shade, the white is reliably pure and brilliant, and the rings are almost never incomplete. The animal is available from any breeder who keeps up on "what's hot" and is know for a remarkably calm temperament and maniacal appetite. It is also easy to breed and the eggs are very hardy,

D. BREIDENBACH

Lampropeltis triangulum smithi (Smith's Milk Snake).

hatching success rate being about 80 %.

Smith's Milk Snake
Lampropeltis trianglum smithi
Williams, 1978
Named in honor of noted herpetologist and good friend Dr. Hobart M. Smith, this beautiful animal can only be reliably distinguished through tedious scale counts. It occurs in a small section of southern Mexico in sectors notably higher in elevation than those of the closeby *L. t. polyzona.* Not much is known about its natural history, but it is believed to inhabit dry arroyos in semiarid

R. MCCARTHY

Lampropeltis triangulum stuarti (Stuart's Milk Snake).

regions and thought to intergrade with *polyzona* regularly, possibly *arcifera* as well.

Stuart's Milk Snake
Lampropeltis triangulum stuarti
Williams, 1978
Another recently described subspecies, this one can easily be identified by the obvious "V" mark on the snout, the color of the marking being basic white laid over dark black. The snake occurs in the dry forests and coastal plains of El Salvador, Honduras, Nicaragua, and N. W. Costa Rica. The young resemble the adults almost exactly,

R. G. MARKEL

Lampropeltis triangulum syspila (Red Milk Snake).

except their overall tint may be a little "brighter." Named after L. C. Stuart, this snake is known to intergrade with *L. t. oligozona* in the Finca La Gloria area of Guatemala. Stuart's Milk Snake is not seen in the hobby.

Red Milk Snake
Lampropeltis triangulum syspila
(Cope, 1888)
Often kept domestically, the Red Milk Snake sometimes commands a high price. Reasons for its popularity probably include the fact that it is easy to breed, can subsist on a diet of pinkie mice, and has a relatively controlled temper. Some

Lampropeltis triangulum taylori (Utah Milk Snake).

specimens have a strong resemblance to the Eastern Milk Snake, *L. t. triangulum*, but *syspila* can be correctly identified by the black band on the posterior portion of the parietals and the broken spots that occur ventrolaterally. The Red Milk Snake rarely grows over three and a half feet and haunts wooded hillsides and rocky regions of Indiana, Kentucky, Oklahoma, and the Dakotas.

Utah Milk Snake
Lampropeltis triangulum taylori
Tanner and Loomis, 1957
W. W. Tanner and R. B. Loomis named this subspecies after noted naturalist Edward H. Taylor in their "Taxonomic and distributional study of the western subspecies of the Milk Snake, *Lampropeltis doliata,*" *Trans. Kansas Acad. Sci. 60:12-42.* The holotype, a female, was collected on May 24th 1951 and is now in the collection at Bringham Young University. The snake can be distinguished by a snout that is almost always entirely black and a ring count of 23 to 34, which is a fairly large number for this species. Not a whole lot is known about *taylori*'s natural history, but it does seem to spend an unusually large amount of time underground and appears to be quite colonial. It is

also believed that it intergrades with *L. t. celaenops* in Conejos County, Colorado.

Eastern Milk Snake
Lampropeltis triangulum triangulum
(Lacepede, 1788)
The nominate subspecies, *L. t. triangulum* is a very hardy and widespread animal, covering a good portion of the East Coast of North America. It is one of the few Milk Snakes that does not bear the blatant red/black/white color pattern scheme, but may instead occur with a ground color of tan, brown, brick red, or ashy gray, with darker saddles or blotches outlined with black or very dark brown. There is an interesting "offshoot" of

Lampropeltis triangulum triangulum (Eastern Milk Snake).

this snake known as *L. t. "temporalis"* (vernacular: the "Coastal Plains" Milk Snake) which some herpetologists believe to be an intergrade between *triangulum* and the Scarlet Kingsnake, *L. (t.) elapsoides*, while others perceive it as a product of the Red Milk Snake, *L. t. syspila*. Finally there are those who downplay the concept of *"temporalis"* altogether and claim it to be nothing more than a simple color variety.

ACQUIRING MILK SNAKES

One of the most fortunate aspects of today's herp hobby, at least from the keeper's perspective, is the fact that the popularity of reptiles and amphibians has grown so much over the last two decades that now there are virtually dozens of outlets where one can acquire specimens. And since Milk Snakes are so incredibly sought-after, they are, of course, among the most often seen for sale. However, anyone interested in these fascinating animals should know a little bit about those sources before actually making any decisions. The two most popular, pet stores and private breeders, are discusses here.

PET STORES

The first and most obvious place to acquire a Milk Snake would be from a pet store. I don't know what the situation is like in other nations, but there aren't many counties left in the Untied States that don't have at least one pet store, and most of them stock at least a few reptiles. Many stores have dedicated entire sections of their floor space to just herps, and if there isn't a shop like this in your immediate area, there's a better than average chance one is not much more than a short drive away.

Once you have found a suitable store, don't just run inside and buy the first Milk Snake you see. In fact, don't be disappointed if there aren't any available at that particular moment. Remember, Milk Snakes are very popular and don't sit in their pet store cages for long. Ask the store owner or manager when he or she plans to get their next order and if there will be any Milk Snakes included. If they say no, perhaps you can inquire about which Milk Snakes they can obtain through custom-ordering. This can sometimes be a risk since you don't really know what you're getting until you see it, but

chances are you won't run into the need to make such a request since almost all pet stores that pride themselves on snake stock are wise enough to carry at least one variety of the the highly popular Milk Snakes.

When you do finally locate a pet store with a Milk Snake for sale, don't just grab it from the tank and hand over the cash. You've got to do some investigation work first; after all, you want to make sure you're getting a

Lampropeltis triangulum triangulum (Eastern Milk Snake). Shown in a plastic jar that can be used for transport or as temporary housing.

first-rate specimen, right? This is not to say that pet stores are horrible places that try to sell off poorly conditioned snakes just to turn a quick buck; that is not true at all. The point is, you as a consumer have a right to be sure the product you are spending your money on is worth the price you're paying. It's no different

SUSAN C. MILLER AND HUGH MILLER

Simple cloth sack for carrying snakes.

burns, etc. Remember, even a Milk Snake that loves to eat can be thrown from its feeding cycle by a bad burn or a mouse bite. Make sure the snake looks like it's in good shape. I'd like to take a moment, however, to say that just because a Milk Snake you're thinking of buying has a few mites or a tick or two, or even a small cut or a light burn, doesn't at all mean its a bad snake and should be turned down. I myself once purchased a pair of Fox Snakes, *Elaphe vulpina*, from a dealer who was having problems curing their mite infestation. Both snakes would eat with great eagerness but the dealer kept them in a back room away from the sales floor because he thought no one would be interested in them. Knowing mites could be cured easily enough (and

than if you're buying a car. If it belches smoke and backfires then you're not going to buy it, right? If a Milk Snake looks genuinely ill or refuses to eat then it's just as bad.

There are a couple of "tests" you can run in order to help you make your judgment. The first is a simple feeding test. Ask the store employees if you can see the snake eat. Let them know you are more than willing to pay for the mouse or lizard you will need in order to run this test. If they tell you the snake has only eaten recently and probably won't be hungry again for a few days, come back in a few days. I have been using this approach for years and believe me, it has saved me from buying a number of "bad" snakes. Remember the first rule of keeping a snake healthy—if it is willing to eat on its own then you're more than halfway down the road to successfully maintaining it. If it won't, you're in deep trouble.

After you've assured yourself that you have a real pig on your hands, take the snake out and give it a thorough lookover. Look for the obvious problems like mites, ticks,

seeing that the problem was not terribly severe) I bought the pair at a good price, brought them home, killed off the offending "bugs," and the very next season the pair bred for me. My point is, if you run across a Milk Snake with some small ailment that you believe can be cured fairly easily, don't let said ailment deter you from acquiring a snake you really want.

Finally, ask the store about their return policy just in case something does go wrong. Of course, in a business like selling animals a store can't give guarantees that stretch into weeks and months, but anywhere from 48 hrs. to one week seems "standard." This helps cover you just in case

SUSAN C MILLER AND HUGH MILLER

Lampropeltis triangulum sinaloae (Sinaloan Milk Snake).

Lampropeltis triangulum hondurensis **(Honduran Milk Snake)**, by Mella Panzella. The Honduran Milk Snake is commonly seen for sale and does quite well in captivity.

something happens that no one, not even the pet store people themselves, could have foreseen.

PROFESSIONAL BREEDERS

Since herpetoculture (a great word for the hobby of keeping and breeding reptiles and amphibians) is becoming quite a sensation, there are more and more private persons turning to it as a relaxing pastime, yearly challenge, and even small business. For those of us who have a fascination for something like the Milk Snakes, this is good news. Not only can it be reliably stated that virtually every snake breeder has at least one Milk Snake variety on his or her current price list, but the very fact that they deal only in captive-bred animals means the specimens they sell will be first-rate.

There are a number of ways an interested party can contact one of these people. Herp magazines, newsletters, and journals all advertise the top breeders, and beyond that

W.P. MARA

Lampropeltis triangulum amaura (Louisiana Milk Snake). Belly pattern of juvenile.

there are a number of secondary sources that you can find out about by looking into one of the aforementioned places (there are, for example, a number of herp directories being offered at the moment). There are also the many herp societies which obviously have many members who breed snakes. So, as you can see, there are quite a few choices at your disposal.

The logical route to follow once you have found an address or phone number for one of these breeders is to ask for his or her most current price list. Nine times out of ten these lists are free (or you will have to supply an SASE, or, at the very least, a very small fee), and will give you all the information you need to know about that particular specialist—what snakes are being bred, what the prices are, shipping and handling information, etc. The other nice thing about the private breeders is that many of them will breed things that you'll never see in pet shops because sometimes they are breeding animals for the very first time. If, for example, someone is running the initial breed for Smith's Milk Snake, *Lampropeltis triangulum smithi*, you are certainly not going to find it anywhere else. And events like this are never kept secret; it would be impossible to miss the classic headlines like "FIRST TIME EVER BRED!" or "NEVER BEFORE

OFFERED FOR SALE!"

The down sides to private breeders, although only small ones at that, involve three things—first of all you have no idea what you've bought until you see it, at which time you may be sorely disappointed. Second, if you are buying top-quality snakes, you will be paying prices in accordance. And finally, shipping snakes is not cheap.

The first problem, buying something without seeing it, can be solved easily enough by asking the breeder if he or she can send you a color photo of "your" specimen. This practice has come heavily into vogue in the last few years and is now considered standard procedure.

The problem with price is not really so much of a stumbling block as it is a decision: are you willing to pay the asking price? The nice aspect of this is of course that you get what you pay for. If you're spending top dollar, you have every right to expect a top snake.

Finally, the only issue that can't be resolved by either seller or buyer is the ludicrous cost of shipping snakes these days. Somewhere along the way the mail system decided it would be best if snakes could only be legally shipped by air freight. The flaw there is that sending a freightful can be awfully frightful (isn't that a great line?). On more than one occasion I have seen a hobbyist pay more in shipping than he or she did for the actual snake!

W. P. MARA

Lampropeltis triangulum gentilis (Central Plains Milk Snake). Captive-bred newborn specimen. Captive-bred Milk Snakes are far superior than those that have been taken from the wild, for many reasons.

Considering how much some snakes cost, that is pretty frightful indeed. There isn't really a heck of a lot you can do about it, either, but if you belong to a herp club or society then perhaps you can interest some of the other members in the stock of the breeder you're buying from. If you can find three or four other people who are interested in something from the same seller, you can ship all your purchases together for the same shipping price and cut the cost between you.

Lampropeltis triangulum annulata (Mexican Milk Snake). A hobbyist should always be sure of what he or she is getting when purchasing a tri-colored Milk Snake. Many of the subspecies look very much alike.

KEN LUCAS

HOUSING MILK SNAKES

For the average keeper, a snake under four or five feet in maximum adult length, of slender build, and requiring low maintenance, is ideal. This is probably one reason the Milk Snakes have been so popular; they fit this description almost perfectly. In regards to housing, the Milk Snakes are a cinch.

SIZE OF THE ENCLOSURE

The cost of purchasing a tank for a large boid like, say, a Reticulated Python, *Python reticulatus*, which will grow to well over 20 feet, can easily be cause for distress. After all, who wants to spend hundreds of dollars just on a tank? The amount of money one could dump into a glass aquarium or a pair of aquariums for a breeding set of these monsters could instead be spent on another breeding pair of Milk Snakes!

But the keeper of Milk Snakes does not have such problems. Even the largest member of the Milk Snake conglomeration, the Ecuadorian Milk Snake, *Lampropeltis triangulum micropholis*, only attains an average maximum adult length of 72in./183 cm. When compared to most other popular hobby snakes, that's not so bad. A

SUSAN C. MILLER AND HUGH MILLER

A basic snake cage, with a spot lamp and a heat pad. Note also the ventilation holes on the sides and the sliding glass front.

keeper could easily house a pair of these in a 30-gallon "long." I myself kept a captive-bred adult pair of magnificent Sinaloan Milk Snakes, *Lampropeltis triangulum sinaloae*, (adult length—48 in./122 cm) in a 20-gallon "long" for a number of years, and even bred them successfully for a number of seasons. (The 20-gallon "long" is one of the commonly seen and easily acquired glass aquariums in the hobby.)

But to return to the original point, a simple guideline to follow concerning the size of your tank in correlation to the size of the snake(s) you have, all you have to do is follow a formula: five gallons of tank size for every foot of snake you have. Thus, a foot-long Milk Snake could live well in a 5-gallon tank, and a four-footer could live in a 20. Up to four snakes at a time would correspond with this formula (meaning you could indeed put four four-foot snakes in a 20-gallon tank), but placing any more than four snakes in a tank at one time is not at all a bright idea, not to mention inhumane.

ACQUIRING TANKS

There are a number of places a

hobbyist can go to acquire his or her snake tanks. The simplest and most obvious is at a pet store. There are a number of wonderful advantages to buying tanks at pet stores, the first being an incredible selection. Not only do most pet stores have dozens of tanks in dozens of shapes and sizes, but if you don't like what's available at that moment you can always custom-order something. Most herpetoculturists are surprised at the vast number of the oddly designed glass aquariums that are manufactured these days, but the fishkeepers aren't. Some of the latter's needs are indeed unique. If you go into a pet store and don't see something you like, ask the manager or owner if you can browse through a catalogue. You may find just what you're looking for. One note of warning, however—custom tanks tend to be a bit expensive, so be prepared.

Another place hobbyists often find tanks are at yard sales, garage sales, and flea markets. The obvious advantage here is that the tanks found in these places will of course be considerably less expensive than new ones. On the other hand, you will not be getting any guarantees

W. P. MARA

For temporary arrangements, a hidebox can be made from a plastic food container with an entrance hole cut at the rim.

that they won't leak, and you certainly won't have a return policy. Furthermore, your choices are instantly limited to whatever happens to be for sale. If you don't like the tank's shape or size, too bad.

If none of this bother you, however, then perhaps you should spend a few weekends scanning newspapers looking for such events. In the United States they seem to be an everyday thing (or I should say an every weekend thing). And I have to be honest—I have found more than my share of fantastic bargains.

Another option, if you have the nerve and don't mind being perceived as a little on the shameless side, is to watch for discarded tanks on the side of the road during the days when your local public maintenance department has their bulk garbage pickup. You'd be amazed how many people will throw away perfectly good glass aquariums simply because they are too dirty or are just taking up space in the garage or attic.

Finally, returning once more to the pet stores, it never hurts to ask if there are any cracked or otherwise slightly damaged tanks lying around. More often than not a shop will have one or two of these that they just don't know what to do with. Usually you will end up paying very little for a tank that just needs a dab of silicone squeezed over a hairline split or maybe has a slow leak in one corner. Of course, there is a limit to how badly a tank can be damaged before it simply becomes trash, but that can be summed up easily enough on sight.

DECORATING A TANK

Milk Snakes are fairly active creatures and would probably be appreciative if you gave them more than just a waterbowl and a cardboard box. Of course, in the interests of making things easy on the keeper (especially the keeper who has a large number of herps) it is best to keep setups simple so that cleaning is not a complete nuisance. That doesn't mean the tank has to look bland, however.

Substrate

Firstly, let's go over the basics. Substrate is a ten-dollar word for cage bedding. Rocks are a substrate, as are wood shavings and newspaper. These days we also have corn cob, pine bark nuggets and pine bark mulch, indoor/outdoor carpeting, and a whole arsenal of other stuff.

But in my many years as a keeper, I have found the absolute

Four Paws Terrarium Linings are fully washable and mildew resistant. The thick grass of the lining provides a happy and healthy environment for small animals.

best cage bedding of all is the good old paper towel. I realize that may not be completely correlative to what I said a moment ago about not wanting a tank to look bland, but one must realize that the material that covers the floor of your snake's tank is what will need to be cleaned most often, so visual aesthetics should be sacrificed here. Rocks, for example, might look nice, but unless you're the type of person who enjoys hernias, I certainly wouldn't advise using them (nothing like carrying thirty pounds of dead weight to a slop sink every few days, huh? You can forget about leaving your spinal cord to science). And wood shavings might be inexpensive and lighter than rocks, but they're also potentially dangerous to your pets and, in my opinion, are messy and visually repulsive. There are negatives to be considered with the other substrates as well, but of course it is ultimately the keeper's choice as to what he or she will use. I have given the one that I still rely on after many years of keeping (and after trying all the others during that time).

Large Rocks

It is always good to have at least one large rock in a Milk Snake's tank, if for no other reason than to provide something rough for the animal to begin a shed on. It always galled me in the past to walk into a pet store and see a snake with no rock or other abrasive surface in its quarters, and of course the animal had either a dried skin stuck to its body, or at the very least multiple patches of such.

Also, some Milk Snake subspecies tend to hide quite a bit (like the popular Scarlet Kingsnake, *Lampropeltis elapsoides*, for example) and thus would welcome something to crawl behind if they feel their hidebox is inadequate.

The Waterbowl

Just grab a bowl from the kitchen cabinet and fill it with water, right? Well, not exactly. A lot of amateur keepers make that mistake, but it's no crime. If you take an ordinary "human's" bowl and place it in a Milk Snake's tank, what happens? The snake leans down on the rim to drink and it tips back, spilling water all over the cage and leaving the snake drenched, thirsty, and probably pretty irritated.

The kind of bowl a snake keeper wants is one that has a base broader than the opening. Rarely, if ever, will you see these advertised as "snake bowls," but they can be found as a dog or cat product. Make sure you purchase one that is fairly good-sized so a snake can bathe in it during a molt cycle and soften its old skin.

Hideboxes

The whole reason a keeper provides one of his or her snakes with a hidebox in the first place is for the purpose of providing the animal with privacy, so choose one that is both dark and fairly tight. A Milk Snake wants to feel like its entire body is totally obscured. A plastic shoebox or one of the many plastic food containers with a hole drilled into the top (rather than through one of the sides) is very effective, but be sure the container is of a solid color and not just simply opaque, so as to assure complete darkness. The reason for the hole in the top is rather simple—the animal feels like it is going "down into" its resting area, thus replicating the same sensation in

Four Paws Safety Screen Covers are designed to fit any size tank. The locking system ensures the pet's safety.

the wild. As minor as this detail may sound, many keepers have found that their snakes react slightly better to captive life when provided with it.

Another small point you may want to consider is lining the floor of the hidebox with paper toweling. This makes the box easier to clean if and when a snake defecates in it.

Branches for Climbing

Generally speaking, Milk Snakes are not great climbers, but on the other hand it would be a lie to say a few tree branches added in to a tank setup would do them any harm. In fact, you many actually discover your snakes crawling about on them every now and again and certainly the exercise won't hurt. The only problem you have to watch out for with wood is its annoying lack of cleanability. Once a snake has defecated on anything wooden, chances are you will have to throw it out because the risk of infestation leading to further, more serious, problems is simply too great. Along the same lines, it is mildly dangerous to import branches from one's yard or a nearby forest because the wood could be infested with one of many harmful parasites. Mites and ticks would be only too glad to abandon a branch in order to jump on a nice fat Milk Snake. Some keepers insist you can clean a wood product covered in snake feces by removing the filth with sandpaper. I suppose this is true to a point, but how many keepers wish to go to that kind of trouble once or twice a week? If you have only one or two tanks it probably isn't so bad, but beyond that it becomes a tedious chore.

CLIMATE CONTROL

As with any herptile, there are multiple aspects of environmental

PHOTO COURTESY ZOO MED

The Repti Therm range of Under Tank Heaters are designed to heat your terrarium a minimum of 5 to 10 degrees warmer than room temperature.

balance to be considered. Heat, for example, is not simply a matter of leaving an animal at room temperature. Lighting plays an important role too; leave a light on for too many or too few hours at the wrong time of year and you may find your females producing nothing but clutches of infertile eggs.

Heat

Depending on where your Milk Snake came from, during the active season it will need an ambient temperature of between 80 and 90°F/26 to 32°C. It would be safe to say all subspecies of *L. triangulum* could thrive at 85°F/ 29°C, but give or take five degrees from that point and you will still be hovering within a safe zone.

There are many ways to provide such temperatures at a hobbyist's disposal these days. One of the more popular is something called the "hot rock." All a hot rock is, in essence, is a molded "stone" with a heating element inside. Once plugged in, most hot rocks generate a heat of around 88 to 92°F/31 to 33°C. One of the nice things about hot rocks is that a snake can climb on and off them at will. Furthermore, hot rocks are inexpensive both at the time of purchase and concerning electrical costs. The bad side of the hot rock is that it can't get wet and its electrical cord has to run out from the tank, which usually means a slight

you throw the pad away with it? I give you a simple solution to all of this right here—the moment you remove the wax label covering the

PHOTO COURTESY ZOO MED

Repticare Rock Heater is designed to duplicate the natural basking process of all lizards and snakes.

sacrifice in tank security.

Another option is the "heating pad." These have become very popular in the modern herp hobby. Heating pads are black (usually) squares of a hard, rubbery material that stick on to the bottom of a glass tank. Much like the hot rocks, they are inexpensive to buy and run. The heat is not high and yet seems perfectly adequate. Also, there is no breach of tank security since the pad is stuck to the outside of the tank. However, a keeper may find the "permanence" of adhering the pad to the tank a little irritating, not to mention impractical. After all, how are you supposed to wash a tank that has an electrical item stuck to the bottom of it? Furthermore, what if you want to put the pad someplace else? Finally, if the tank gets ruined somehow, do

sticky side of the pad, wrap the entire pad in tin foil. Then, simply slide it under whatever tank you wish to use it with.

Finally, if you have a large number of tanks and supplying each one with a hot rock or a heating pad is just too cost-ridiculous, you can always use the old standby method and simply heat the entire room. Of course, this could be rather expensive, depending on the circumstances. Remember your temperature: between 80 and 90°F/ 27 to 32°C. If the room cannot attain this gradient on its own you will have to purchase a separate heating appliance. There are a great number of heaters on the market, but the best kind for this purpose are called "ceramic" heaters. Since they are so efficient, a keeper will encounter notable savings on his or her electric bill compared with the bill you'd have if you used a "standard"-type electric heater. Also, ceramic heaters are not generally expensive to begin with. It's also worth mentioning that almost all models have a built in thermostat, but be careful—some of them draw a lot of energy, so make sure your outlet can handle it. If you feel the cord getting too warm, spend the money and have an electrician come in and install a heavy-duty outlet. It's a lot cheaper than rebuilding the whole house or apartment after the place has burned down.

Lighting

In regards to lighting the tank of a Milk Snake, let's use the word "photoperiod," exclusively. In essence, photoperiod is the amount of time in which a Milk Snake's light is left on. For example, a snake with a photoperiod of 12 hours has its lights left on for 12 hours everyday. Simple, right?

Yes, but the effect is has on the animal is not so simple. In the wild, the amount of light a snake receives tells it a lot about what season its in. Snakes have a natural sense of this and depend on the changes to dictate which cycles they are experiencing. Thus, it is the keeper's job to re-create the correct photoperiods in captivity.

What you need is a simple timer

The Reptile Brightlight Heat Lamp provides purified full spectrum daylight that simulates the natural photoenvironment of the reptiles habitat.

device that can be plugged into any ordinary wall socket and then connected to your lighting apparatus. As the seasons change you will have to adjust the timer settings. Of course, in the winter when the snakes are hibernating you will not be giving them any light at all, but in the spring and fall the "days" will be shorter than in the summer.

The only other aspect of artificial lighting that a keeper might be concerned with is the nutritional quality of the light being used. Lizard and turtle enthusiasts should know what that means; some forms of light (known in broad terms as "full-spectrum" light) actually have nutritional qualities that these two herp groups need in order to survive. In short, full-spectrum lighting triggers calcium-producing enzymes that encourage proper bone growth.

However, snakes are spared this need and thus such lights are not necessary; the nutrients are acquired in their diet. It is perhaps most fortunate for the keeper that this is the case, as most full-spectrum bulbs are frighteningly expensive. It should be pointed out, though, that many professional keepers claim to get better breeding results from snakes that have been exposed to full-spectrum lighting, so it is something a hobbyist should consider.

Humidity and Moisture

For the most part, Milk Snakes do not need a very moist or humid environment. Some amphibians, for example, need daily tank mistings and a damp substrate. This is not the case with Milk Snake specimens, but since there are so many different Milk Snake varieties, and from so many different locales, the best thing a keeper can do is garner some information about the his or her own particular animal's natural environment and go from there. If such data are not available to you, however, you can get by with a dry tank (no mistings or damp substrate) or, for more tropical subspecies, one that is only slightly humid.

PHOTO COURTESY ZOO MED

Repticare® Ceramic Heat Emitters produce heat with no visible light for all types of reptile, amphibian and plant terrariums.

TANK CLEANING

Although we would all like to be able to keep our Milk Snakes's tanks clean without physically overexerting ourselves , there will be times when thorough cleanings will be called for. This means heavy tanks will have to be carefully lifted and moved about, cage implements will have to be removed (as well as the occupants), and so on.

To make the task as easy for you as possible, I am including a simple step-by-step system that I have been using for years and has produced great results.

1) **Remove the snakes and put them in a secure temporary container.** Almost anything will do. I use 10-gallon spackle buckets, but that's just a personal preference. The main concern is, again, the security.

2) **Remove all cage implements.** Throw out those that are disposable, and place the reusable ones (plastic hideboxes, rocks, etc.) aside for later cleaning.

3) **Fill the tank with warm water, soap, and a little bleach.** A few people may claim that bleach is dangerous in conjunction with any facet of herpetocultural husbandry, but a little bit goes a long way and such claims are utter nonsense.

Scrub the tank well (although be careful of highly abrasive pads—you don't want to scratch the glass) and make sure you get all the corners and so forth.

4) **Rinse in cold water.** And rinse more than once. Make sure the water runs clear through every part of the tank. Even the slightest trace of bleach or soap will cause a Milk Snake great irritation. The rinsing stage is very important to the safety of your pets.

5) **Wash and rinse the reusable cage implements in the same manner as you did the tank.**

6) **Dry everything thoroughly.**

7) **Replace and reset everything in the tank.** And don't be afraid to arrange the tank a little differently each time. The snake(s) won't mind.

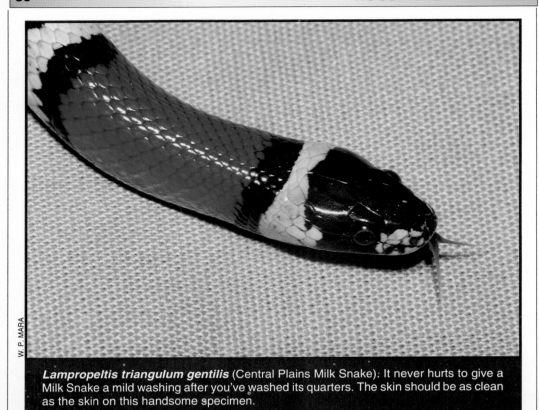

Lampropeltis triangulum gentilis (Central Plains Milk Snake): It never hurts to give a Milk Snake a mild washing after you've washed its quarters. The skin should be as clean as the skin on this handsome specimen.

8) **Bathe the snakes.** That's right, give them quick, mild baths. Why? Because if their tank was dirty, they just might be dirty too. Of course, you won't be washing them the same way you washed everything else. A few moments under lukewarm water, rubbing them thoroughly with a washcloth, and then drying them off gently with a soft towel is all that's required.

9) **Replace snakes, replace top, and you're done.**

As you can see, this system is simple and efficient, and can be performed in most any household. A further note of advice is that you should set up some sort of routine schedule and stick to it. A tank should never remain dirty for too long; I used to clean my tanks once every week whether I thought they really needed it or not. A lot can happen in that length of time, and diseases can run rampant if given an unclean tank to thrive in. The best thing you can do to avoid health problems is give proper attention to sanitation.

FEEDING MILK SNAKES

It has always been my personal opinion that the only aspect of serpentine husbandry a keeper truly has to worry about is feeding. I base this motto on one simple concept—you can completely control every other part of a snake's captive life, but if it does not wish to eat, you are in trouble. You can keep a Milk Snake warm or cold, give it light or darkness, and with a little discipline and hard work, always provide quarters that are sparkling clean, but you can't make it eat if it doesn't want to. (You can of course force-feed it, but that's not really much of a life and certainly not what is desired. When it comes to this point you no longer have a pet, but a prisoner.)

There are a whole array of reasons why a Milk Snake may become a fussy feeder, so it is important that you gain a better understanding of the subtleties involved in snake feeding. It will help you avoid many unpleasantries in the future.

are excellent meals for Milk Snakes. They are relatively inexpensive and can even be bred by the keeper if he or she wishes. The most rational way to go about such an endeavor is by setting up a series of 10-gallon (mice) or 20-gallon (rats) tanks with a thick bedding of wood shavings, a water bottle, a daily allowance of bird seed and dried dog food, and a breeding quartet of one male to three females in each. This is the approach I subscribed to for years with great success. If you try it yourself you may find a fascination for the remarkable gestation rate of these tiny creatures—every 21 and 22 days for mice and rats respectively, meaning every three weeks you will have a new litter of Milk Snake food.

Mice probably are the food item most often given to captive Milk Snakes. Photo by Michael Gilroy.

FOOD CHOICES

The first and most obvious consideration is choice of food. There are a number of items Milk Snakes will accept for a meal, but some are less practical for the keeper than others.

Mice and Rats

We'll start with what are probably the most common of all colubrid foods—mice and rats. These small mammals can be obtained at nearly any pet store that sells herptiles and

One of the most hotly debated issues in herpetoculture over the last few years has been the question of whether or not a snake's mice or rats should be offered dead or alive. Many professional breeders choose the former and train their stock to take everything pre-killed. The reasons seem logical enough—a hungry rat or mouse placed in a tank with a not-so-hungry snake could easily end up being the hunter rather than the hunted.

But I have to confess that I

disagree with this approach nevertheless and have never trained any of my snakes to take dead food. I only feed them during times when I am free and thus am always nearby if any problems occur. The final decision as to which method you choose to utilize will of course be up to you and you alone.

Lizards

Another dietary item commonly accepted by Milk Snakes is their close relative the lizard. Speaking nutritionally, lizards are a perfectly acceptable meal, and in some places you can probably catch them with regularity.

But there are some problems. One involves the keeper's conscience. Many hobbyists do not like the idea of using other herptiles as food. Another problem is cost potential; what if you can't find lizards nearby and you have to go buy some? That can be very expensive.

Finally, do your really want a snake that only eats lizards in the first place? If you can wean the animal onto mice, then continually giving it saurians won't help.

The bottom line is, if you can supply lizards to your Milk Snakes on a steady basis without driving yourself into debt then the idea really isn't so bad, but chances are there are not a lot of hobbyists who fall into that category. The solutions? Weaning these types of Milk Snakes onto mice or simply not keeping such snakes to begin with.

Other Snakes

Here we have the same problem as we had with lizards, but there is an added catch—many Milk Snakes prey on other snakes almost exclusively. The Scarlet Kingsnake, *Lampropeltis telapsoides*, for example, might take a small pinkie if you're lucky, but it will

HORST MAYER

"Pinkies" are available at most pet stores and make a good meal for young Milk Snakes.

go after a little Ringneck Snake, *Diadophis punctatus*, anytime and would thank you for it afterward if it could. Scarlet Kings are notorious lizard-eaters as well, which makes matters even more difficult.

So then the real question is, what if you find yourself in possession of one of these infernal reptile-eating Milk Snakes? Is there anything you can do? Sadly, the answer is not really. The only true choice at your disposal is to force-feed the animal pinkie mice until it starts liking them instead. The problem with that is it may take a long, long time, and often the snake will die from stress long before that day comes. The real solution to the problem is just avoid acquiring these types of Milk Snakes in the first place. Again, if you can supply small snakes for food without any problem, then there's really no harm done, but chances are this won't be the case.

MICHAEL GILROY

Many Milk Snake keepers choose to breed their own mice, but that can require a lot of time and trouble.

Birds and Bird Eggs

Finally, there is a minor percentage of Milk Snakes that may accept small birds and/or small bird eggs. And the truth of the matter is, a bird or a bird egg every now and again is, nutritionally speaking, not at all a bad meal for a Milk Snake. If you happen to have access to such items then it is advised that you offer them. If not, you can always find a local aviculturist and ask to buy some small eggs. It has been my experience that young birds and bird eggs are not usually expensive either, depending of course on the species, but the Milk Snakes certainly won't care either way.

TIME OF DAY, HOW MUCH, AND HOW OFTEN

Some keepers wonder what time of day is best for a Milk Snake to eat.

Indeed, I myself have kept specimens which seemed totally disinterested in food items during the morning hours only to go "prowling about" for those same items later that night.

The real answer is that it varies from specimen to specimen, so you will have to experiment with your own to find out. Correct time of day plays in large role with some snakes and yet means nothing to others, so just because the Milk Snake you bought refuses to eat every time you drop in a mouse before you go to work doesn't necessarily mean it will have to be force-fed.

As for how much food a Milk Snake should be given, that judgment is usually made for you by the snake itself! Most Milk Snakes (not all, but most) will simply stop accepting food once they feel they are full. The piggish tendency for a snake to simply eat and eat until it is so full it looks like an overpacked sausage is seen more often in Natricines (garter snakes, water snakes) and other such feisty serpents, but not so much in Milk Snakes.

However, if you do end up with a *triangulum* that just can't seem to get enough (and honestly, who would mind that?), then you will have to rely on your own instinctive judgement because overfeeding a snake is a lot more dangerous than most keepers imagine. Even the largest Milk Snake should only have two or three adult mice per meal, and young that are small enough to take pinkies should never have more than two or three either. Giving them so much food that they throw it up is not only a waste of food, it also risks internal damage and causes the animal unnecessary stress.

How often a Milk Snake should be fed depends on a number of things, and again your natural instincts must sum up the final answer. How much does it eat each time? Obviously snakes that eat two large mice per feeding will not have to be fed as often as those that eat just one. How active is the snake's metabolism? Does it defecate every two days, or every four? Generally speaking, I always fed my Milk Snakes every five days and this seemed to suit them fine. Any earlier

dangerous) is the former and will be the one discussed in this book. For it to be done properly, you should begin by acquiring the correct equipment:

1) A force-feeding syringe, available in any well-stocked drugstore. If you can't find one in stock, acquire one from a surgical supply house.

2) Lengths of plastic tubing of varying widths, to be attached to the

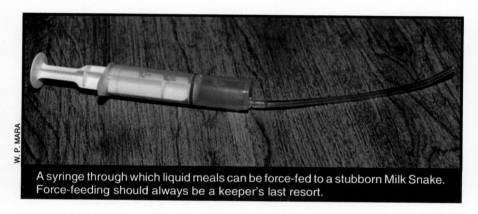

A syringe through which liquid meals can be force-fed to a stubborn Milk Snake. Force-feeding should always be a keeper's last resort.

than every four is simply too soon and anymore than every eight seems to indicate you just want to keep them alive and nothing more.

FORCE-FEEDING

There is perhaps no greater nightmare a keeper can experience force-feeding one of his or her snakes. It speaks volumes about that particular snake's faring in captivity. It is unhealthy, unhappy, and, if you have to do it regularly, the snake very probably is not going live. But sometimes it's necessary, and therefore a keeper should be well-informed of the correct procedures involved since incorrect actions can result in injuries and occasional deaths.

There are two types of force-feeding—liquid via a tube, and with the use of actual bulk foods (dead mice, strips of meat, etc.). The most common (and in my opinion the least

end of the syringe. Aquarium tubing can be used for most larger specimens, but with smaller snakes you will again have to go to a surgical supply store.

3) Some harmless lubricant to be used on the end of the tubing so as to slide it down the snake's throat easier. I have always relied on vegetable oil.

Once you have gathered all the necessary paraphernalia, you need to become acquainted with a liquid "recipe" of sorts that will provide a Milk Snake with all the nutrients it is missing by not eating. I have used a combination of raw egg, a small amount of lean hamburger meat, and a pinch of multi-vitamin powder, mixed into a fine liquid in a blender and then strained so as to filter out any excess suet, etc., left behind by the hamburger meat. Of course, a keeper can use whatever food mixture he or she feels will do the job.

It is very important to remember that this liquid must be given warm, so you may have to place it in a microwave oven for a moment or two. Taking a cold egg and some cold hamburger meat straight from a refrigerator, mixing it, then force-feeding it is very dangerous.

The standard procedure for tube-feeding has been fine-tuned to a great degree through time, and is now considered quite safe and reliable:

1) First, be sure the length of plastic tubing on the end of the syringe is at least two feet long. The reason for all the excess length is to accommodate the keeper. Many hobbyists will only leave a tube of about six inches only to find that while they are trying to insert the tube into the snake's mouth, the weight of the dangling syringe is working against them. With excess tubing, you can rest the syringe on a nearby surface.

Also, cut the end of the tube at a sharp angle so it is easier to slip into the snake's mouth. This simple idea eliminates the normal need for the small "bar" used to pry the snake's mouth open.

2) Work from a table or other flat surface. Don't waste your time trying to hold the snake in one hand and

Four Paws Nature's Reptile Vita-Spray was formulated by veterinarians and herpetologists and contains essential vitramins that are important for "reptile health."

manipulate the tube and syringe in the other while you're standing. Remember, all you have to be concerned with at the beginning is getting the tube into the snake's throat, so all you're really dealing with is the snake's head and the tip of the tube. Resting both the syringe and the snake's body on a flat surface with help you avoid a lot of unnecessary frustration.

3) Now you're ready to force-feed. The first step is to fill the syringe with the warmed liquid mixture. This is easy enough: simply place the tube into the container and pull back the plunger. Do the best you can to avoid getting air bubbles in the syringe body and don't be afraid to fill the body of the syringe to its maximum. This does not mean you have to use all of it.

4) Now for the hard part—getting to tube into the snake's mouth. The key here is to be firm enough with the snake's head and yet gentle enough so as not to cause an injury. Doing this correctly takes a lot of confidence and a pair of steady hands, so don't let your nerves get to you. Grasp the animal with your thumb on its head and your other fingers wrapped around its chin and neck, then take the end of the tube, dip it in the inert lubricant, and pry the snake's mouth open. Once you have done this, gently slide the tube

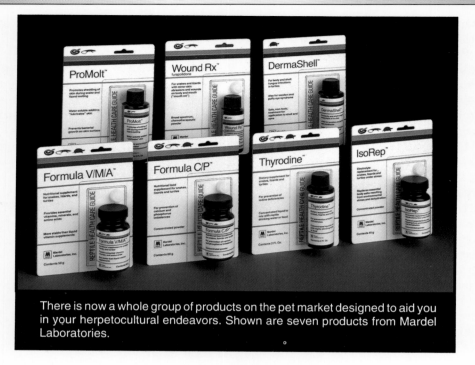

There is now a whole group of products on the pet market designed to aid you in your herpetocultural endeavors. Shown are seven products from Mardel Laboratories.

down the snake's throat, keeping in mind that it does not have to be slid down very far. Depending on the size of the Milk Snake, it is not necessary to go down any further than an inch or two beyond the point where the upper and lower jaws meet.

5) Once the tube is in place, squeeze the snake's two jaws together just enough to keep the tube secure, then, with your free hand, pick up the syringe and begin pressing down on the plunger. The amount of liquid mixture you give the animal should be equal about half in bulk of what it normally eats. Remember, force-feeding is only a temporary measure and not a substitute for normal feeding. A further point that must not be forgotten is that the plunger must be pressed down *slowly*. If it is done

in a rush the liquid is guaranteed to come right back up.

6) Once you are finished, pull the tube back out very slowly and gently place the snake back into its quarters. Then squirt the rest of the mixture into a garbage can and wash the syringe and tubing out immediately by placing the tube in a small bowl of cold water and pulling and pushing the plunger back and forth until all the parts appear clean. If you wait too long to do this the excess liquid mixture will dry up and the syringe and tubing will very probably have to be replaced.

It goes without saying the snake will be highly stressed after this procedure and should be left alone for at least three days.

BREEDING MILK SNAKES

One of the main reasons Milk Snakes have always been so popular in the herp hobby is because they are so easy to breed. In fact, many an experienced keeper can claim that his or her first breeding success was with some variant of the *Lampropeltis triangulum* group.

The procedures are fairly simple, but the keeper still has to be willing to spend the time and have the patience to execute everything correctly. It would be misleading to say breeding any snake is *easy*, but few are as close to easy as the Milk Snakes.

WILLIAM B. ALLEN, JR

Lampropeltis triangulum triangulum (Eastern Milk Snake). One of the most appealing aspects of the Milk Snakes is the fact that they are fairly easy to breed. With patience and careful attention, even a beginner can do it.

naturally experience a harsher cold season than its tropical sister the Sinaloan Milk Snake, *L. t. sinaloae*.

Whatever the details may be, the keeper has to be able to re-create this in captivity if successful propagation is to be expected, and the most difficult part of that procedure is maintaining the correct temperatures.

Naturally you are going to have to find out exactly what those temperatures are for the snakes you have, but if this proves difficult, a "general" number of 55°F/13°C seems to work for all Milk Snake sub-species. I myself have hiber-nated both tropical and temperate Milk Snakes at this temperature without any trouble.

Another concern is recognizing which snakes are healthy enough to sustain the trials of hibernation and which aren't. Generally speaking, those specimens which look plump and well-fed are prime candidates whereas those that the keeper knows have not eaten well and look scrawny and undernourished should probably be kept warm all year long, as well as (of course)

HIBERNATION

In relation to where they occur geographically, all Milk Snakes must go through a period of "rest" before they can be expected to reproduce. Of course, some subspecies will have a milder form of hibernation than others. The basic theory states that the more southerly ranging a snake is the gentler its "winter" will be, i.e., the Eastern Milk Snake, *L. t. triangulum*, which occurs primarily in the northeast corner of the United States and into Canada, will those that you know to be suffering from some ailment such as mouth rot, a mite infestation, or whatever.

The first step to artificial hibernation is correct preparation. Milk Snakes do not simply decide it is time to hibernate one day and just crawl into a burrow and go to sleep; it is a gradual process. The main

their ambient temperature, and the key is to do this gradually. A snake that is propelled abruptly into a cold environment will fall into shock and may die. Begin by dropping the temperature about five degrees every day until the desired number is reached.

When hibernating, Milk Snakes

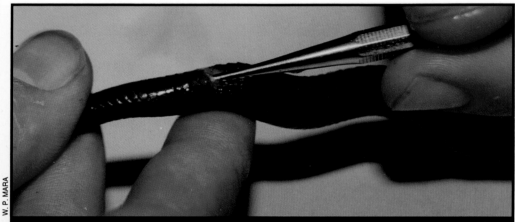

W. P. MARA

Probing a snake is a very delicate affair. If you are not experienced with this facet of snake-keeping, let it be done by someone who is. Careless probing can cause permanent damage to a snake's reproductive organs.

concern a keeper has is making sure his or her snakes have no remaining waste in their systems. If a Milk Snake is placed into hibernation with a full intestine, the feces will ferment in a very short time, damage the intestinal walls, and the snake will die.

Preventing this is not at all difficult. The idea is to stop feeding the snakes you plan to hibernate about three weeks before they are scheduled to be "put down." Then, once a day for the last week they are active, they should be given a three-hour bath in warm water. This will help "loosen and flush out" all remaining wastes.

After you are satisfied your Milk Snakes are fully "emptied out," the next step is to then begin lowering

should be left in the dark and totally undisturbed. Thus, virtually all keepers place them in separate containers. These need not be elaborate or fancy; the professional breeders I know always use glass tanks or plastic shoeboxes. The substrate used most often is soft soil or wood shavings, piled thick enough so the snakes can burrow deep. A three-or four-inch layer is sufficient. A waterbowl should be included as well, and changed every week. Most people think snakes are totally inactive during this time, but this is not the case. They do indeed move about, albeit very slowly, and often appreciate a drink of water.

If you live in an area of the world where it does not get cold enough in the winter to effectively hibernate

Milk Snakes, you may have to forget about hibernating them altogether. Creating the temperatures artificially can be very, very expensive. The only method I am aware of that is used with any regularity is to place the animals in a refrigerator, but even most standard models don't warm up to built-in thermostats, in which case the above mentioned instrument is not necessary. The point is, it is easier to pull low temperatures up rather than vice-versa.

Now that your Milk Snakes are in their artificial hibernaculums, have empty stomachs, and are surrounded by the perfect

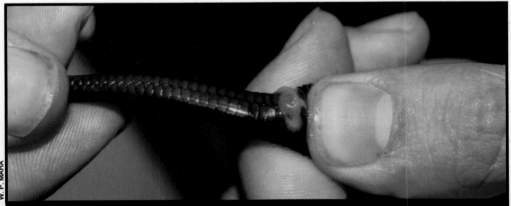

W. P. MARA

"Popping" is another common technique for separating the males from the females, but it is not as reliable as probing and often produces very angry snakes.

55°F/13°F. There are commercially sold champagne refrigerators that can be set to this level, and I'm sure there are others as well, but the cost will be astounding.

On the other hand, if the winters in your locale are somewhat harsh and you fear the temperatures might drop too low, you can always buy a heater and a plug-in thermostat. The latter is a device commonly sold in the better hardware stores and home improvement centers. It can be plugged into any ordinary wall socket, then has an outlet on the back of its own plug where the heater plugs in. There will be a dial on the unit itself which can be set according to what temperature you want to keep the room at. When the temperature dips below that point, the heater will turn on. Of course, many heaters today already have

temperature, there is the question of how long they should be left there. The whole purpose of hibernation is to sort of "reset" the snakes's reproductive hormones, and in most cases a period of two months (eight to nine weeks) will do the trick. Some breeders I have spoken with insist they can get their stock ready in six weeks, but I prefer not to take such chances. The two week difference doesn't matter to the keeper so why risk failure? Count on eight to nine weeks, checking them once a week to ensure they are still in good health (and to change their water), then they will be ready to breed for you.

Taking them out of hibernation is the same as putting them in—it should be done slowly. Give them about three or four more days after they have been reintroduced to their

LUDWIG TRUTNAU

Lampropeltis triangulum sinaloae (Sinaloan Milk Snake). Mother wrapped around a clutch of freshly laid eggs. After egglaying, a mother should be left alone for a day or two.

normal temperature before you try feeding them. They will be groggy and disoriented at first, but in time they will snap back into their old routine.

MATING

Once your Milk Snakes have been properly hibernated and returned to normal activity, the first step toward mating them is segregating the males from the females. Many keepers prefer to do this even during hibernation, but it has been my experience that there is virtually no difference either way.

Once the adults have gotten back into their normal routine of eating, etc., you can begin actually mating them. It has been theorized that it is better to introduce a female into a males tank rather than vice-versa. I must agree. There have been many horror stories concerning male Milk Snakes being eaten by females who apparently felt their territory was being invaded, but few when the males were the host. These subtleties must be observed carefully.

It is important that the keeper remain closeby after he or she has placed the female into the male's tank. Often only one of the adults will be interested in mating, and in such instances it is best to simply separate the pair and try again at a another time. It is not at all unusual for a disinterested Milk Snake to lash out at his or her aggressor after being "worked on" for a while. The normal amount of time the keeper should allow before giving up and separating a pair is about two or three hours.

If on the other hand your pair are receptive to one another, they could remain "locked together" for anywhere from fifteen minutes to four hours. This is one of the more interesting aspects of snake breeding; it is hardly an alacritic process. What usually happens is a male Milk Snake will take immediate notice of a newly introduced female and begin flicking his tongue toward her. He will slide over and begin moving on and around her body. His actions will likely become sharper and more pronounced as his determination grows. Then he will climb on top of her and begin entwining their tails together, lining up the vents so to join in copulation. Once the male has successfully inserted one of his two hemipenes, the pair may remain stationary for the rest of the process. However, a female may also become bored after a time and begin slithering off. During such occurrences the male will very likely bite down on the

female's head and neck, presumably to hold on, but also to let her know he is still there.

Once the mate has concluded, remove the female and place her back into her original quarters. If she has been housed with other females up to this point, set up another tank specifically for her, as privacy is very important during this time. If you wish, you can place the female with the same male (or with other males) a few more times during the next three weeks. This is done to ensure fertility because pregnancy is not always guaranteed. It is always a good idea to breed a female more than once during a season.

GESTATION

The normal gestation period for most *Lampropeltis triangulum* is somewhere in the neighborhood of eight weeks, give or take a week or so. After about the sixth week you will see the female start to swell up and some of her habits will begin to change. It is not at all unusual for a pregnant Milk Snake to lose all interest in food, for example, but whatever you do, don't force-feed them if this happens. Handling pregnant snakes is a very dangerous practice and force-feeding them causes unnecessary stress that could very easily lead to premature egglaying. Only force-feed a pregnant snake if you feel it is severely in need of nutrition, virtually to the point of life or death.

Also, you may find your normally calm and reserved female Milk Snake has decided it doesn't care for your company any longer and will snap at you every time you walk by. This is also quite normal as many pregnant snakes begin to grow edgy as the strains of pregnancy take their toll. This does not mean the animal has been mentally altered for life; once the eggs are laid and the animal is back to peak health it will return to its normally rational self.

EGGLAYING

By the end of the sixth week you will want to start preparing for the laying of the eggs, and the first thing that needs to be done is for you to provide a nesting box. In herpetoculture today, the trend is to use clear (or opaque—it doesn't really matter) plastic shoeboxes with tiny holes drilled in the top to allow air to pass though freely. It has been my experience that these are indeed perfect nesting and incubation boxes. It is advised that you purchase two of these containers at a time—one to drill the small holes in (for incubation), and one to cut a large hole in (so the female has access for nesting). This way, you can simply change the tops after the eggs have been laid, rather than lift the eggs out and risk dropping or "spinning" any of them.

Fill the box with either thickly granulated vermiculite or heavy sphagnum moss (which can be based with sterile potting soil if you wish). Moisten either of these (whichever you choose to use) to the point where it is damp, but certainly not wet. Both of these mediums have proven themselves worthy time and time again so I see no point in suggesting anything else. Simply place the nesting box into the tank and wait. When the time is right, the female will crawl into it and lay her eggs, probably wrapping around them afterward. It is always best that these eggs be removed as soon as possible because Milk Snakes do occasionally eat eggs and after a time may "forget" that the ones in her tank are their own. The lid of the nesting box must be lifted and the female removed very carefully. If this is done recklessly, a female could very well "freak out" under a moment of stress (they are *very* nervy after laying eggs) and start thrashing about, doing irreparable damage to the eggs in the process.

Once the female is out of the box and back in her quarters she should be left alone for at least three days. Then the keeper can try feeding her, keeping in mind that she will very probably be emaciated and should be worked back up to her normal weight as soon as possible.

CARE OF THE EGGS/INCUBATION

After removing the nesting box, take the "nesting" lid from the container and replace it with the "incubating" lid. This second lid should only have a few small holes drilled into it just to allow the passage of fresh air. If there are too many holes, or if the holes are too wide, the incubation medium will dry up quickly and the eggs may spoil (not to mention, if the young do hatch, they will find wide holes a welcome means of escape).

Sometimes a Milk Snake will lay her eggs in a clump rather than individually. If this is the case, you may be able to separate them, provided the laying occurred within the previous 30 minutes or so. Snake eggs dry up rather fast and will adhere strongly to each other, but if they still have a sheen to them, you can very carefully try to separate each one. Keep in mind that if any egg gives any resistance, leave it alone. This is purely a luxurious measure, not a necessity. The theory behind this states simply that if an egg in a clump goes bad it may infect the other eggs touching it. This is not always the case, but having each egg separate is always preferable.

It is worth noting that any eggs laid separate should be marked on the top with a water-based pen. This is done so you can reposition them in the event of any mishaps. Unlike bird eggs, snake eggs cannot be turned during the incubation process or else the yolk will fall on the developing embryo and smother it. Snake eggs must sit in the exact same position they were laid.

The incubation medium should be checked every few days to ensure moisture. If the keeper feels it is becoming too dry, he or she can spray it with a misting bottle. The eggs themselves should not be sprayed, as too much water will damage them. It is understandable that some small water drops will inevitably come in contact with the shells, but this will not do any harm as long as it's kept to an absolute minimum.

The normal incubation time for Milk Snake eggs is anywhere from seven to nine weeks. Ambient temperature can range from ᵗᵒ to 90°F/18 to 32°C, but these are extremes. The number you are looking for is about 80°F/26°C. There have been a number of studies showing a clear effect on both length of incubation and sex determination in relation to temperature. Generally speaking, eggs that are incubated at higher temperatures produce more males and hatch quicker. Thus, at lower temperatures a larger percentage of the neonates will be female but the eggs will take a little longer to hatch.

Although not totally reliable, this fascinating little detail could play a huge role in the advancement of captive-breeding. A breeder could conceivably "hatch to order," thus producing equal numbers of males and females, or, even better, a slightly larger number of females, all of which could of course bear eggs in adulthood. In this day and age when conservation is such a crucial issue and more and more animals are being "saved" in captivity, such information is quite valuable.

The difference between a fertile snake egg and a spoiled one is often very obvious. A rotting snake egg will soon turn yellow and develop a light fungus.

W. P. MARA

HATCHING TIME/CARE OF THE YOUNG

A lot of keepers think that once their eggs have hatched, the seasonal Milk Snake breeding process is over with, but in fact the real work is only just beginning. Proper care of the young is often the most difficult and trying part of the process. Why? Because neonatal Milk Snakes can be very difficult animals to deal with.

You will know when the eggs have hatched either by seeing the newborn snakes slithering about in the egg box or by at least seeing their little snouts peeking up through the slit shell. If you are fortunate enough to be around when the snakes first cut through, you might want to take a close look at one of their snouts through a magnifying glass—there will be a very tiny egg tooth protruding downward from the upper lip. It will be shaped more or less like a triangle, and its function is to help the young snake cut through the leathery egg material. The tooth exists only for this function alone and will drop off within an hour or so.

Once the snakes have revealed themselves you will notice the umbilical cord still attached to their abdomen, then leading back into the shell. Some amateurs feel a strange urge to cut this, but *do not*. In simple words, cutting this cord will kill the snake. Nature has been taking care of this problem for millions of years; the cord will fall off on its own.

When the cord finally falls off (then dries up and deteriorates) and the snakes have left their shells completely, set them up in their own tanks immediately. If you can afford the expense, each snake should be housed individually. Since neonatal Milk Snakes are quite small, the housings need not be very large. Some keepers like to place them in large glass jars. I prefer to put each one in a plastic shoebox, holding the lids down tight with rubber bands wrapped around the whole container, and again I drill some tiny (very tiny) holes for air. The reason for the segregation is obvious—Milk Snakes have been known to eat other Milk Snakes, and the young are particularly aggressive. It's just not worth taking the risk.

The young snakes will need a shallow waterbowl, a dark hidebox, and a rock to shed on, which they will do about a week after they are born. Soft paper toweling is a safe

WILLIAM B. ALLEN, JR.

Lampropeltis triangulum triangulum (Eastern Milk Snake). The moment every breeder waits for—a healthy neonate cutting its way through its leathery shell.

K. T. NEMURAS

Lampropeltis triangulum campbelli (Pueblan Milk Snake). If a neonatal Milk Snake refuses to leave its shell right away, leave it alone. It will come out eventually.

substrate for these tiny little serpents and is highly recommended. After their first shed, you can begin feeding. First, try a pinkie mouse, then a tiny lizard. If all these items fail to arouse interest, you may have to find some tiny snakes (Ringnecks, Brown Snakes, Worm Snakes, etc.). If a snake is stubborn and refuses to feed altogether, you can force-feed it with mouse tails. These should be dipped in vegetable oil at the thicker end, then slid down the young snake's throat by gently spinning as you are pushing. You will be sort of "screwing" the mouse tail into the snake. Once the tail is about halfway down, set the snake in its tank and let it do the rest. Nine times out of ten the animal will cooperate.

DISEASES OF MILK SNAKES

Regardless of how much effort a herpetoculturist puts toward keeping his or her stock free of sickness and disease, there nevertheless will be times when they will be called upon to take action against some form of illness. Snakes are particularly susceptible to disease, but the Milk Snakes are probably among the hardier serpents. Even so, a keeper who prides himself or herself on acquired knowledge and expertise should have some idea of how to diagnose ailments in their earliest stages and then know what to do about them. This is not to say you should then consider yourself a junior veterinarian, but knowing *when* to take your Milk Snake to a professional is often half the battle.

PREVENTIVE MEDICINE

Perhaps the easiest and most effective remedy an ordinary keeper can perform is the one that diverts a problem to begin with. In my opinion, the first level of this is attention to cleanliness. In an earlier chapter I discussed a simple and reliable method for keeping your Milk Snakes and their tanks clean. However, the discipline required to use this technique on a regular basis comes purely from within you. You must ask yourself before you even acquire a Milk Snake, am I willing to take on such a responsibility? You must be honest with your answer. Snakes are not as easy to care for as some people imagine. You *must* keep them clean. That is the first rule of preventive medicine.

The second is feeding. Have you ever gone into a pet store and seen tank after tank of skinny, unhealthy snakes? Often this is because a pet store owner or manager, not wanting to waste too many mice, goldfish, or crickets as food items when they could be selling them for profit, will allow their snakes to go without meals for as long as possible. While it is true that most snakes can live quite well on one or two meals a week, Giving them just enough to survive is simply wrong. They should not be *surviving* in captivity, they should be *thriving*; there is a difference. Therefore, again, if you do not wish to take on the financial responsibility of providing food on its required schedule, then don't keep a Milk Snake at all.

Finally, there are all the other tiny details concerning a Milk Snake's health that could lead to problems if not handled correctly. Handling, for example. If a Milk Snake is handled too often or too roughly it could very easily become stressed (and this of course applies double for pregnant mothers). Improper heating and/or lighting is also a threat. If the surrounding temperature is too high or to low, or if the photoperiod is just plain wrong, you could break a Milk Snake's feeding cycle or throw it into premature hibernation. It all comes down to judgment on the keeper's part. You must develop an instinct for what situations will lessen your snakes's health and then avoid those situations vigorously.

COMMON DISEASES AND SUGGESTED TREATMENTS

Stress

This is perhaps the most subtle and yet one of the deadliest of all snake diseases, and Milk Snakes are certainly not immune. Too many people think of stress as something that attacks only humans, but this is not the case at all. Just because a snake cannot voice its mental suffering doesn't mean it doesn't feel any. Snakes, in fact, are among the most sensitive animals and probably not really cut out for captive life to begin with. They are certainly not as adaptable to domesticity as cats and dogs are.

The origins of stress are multiple, and the signs are, as I said, often very subtle; too subtle, in fact, to notice unless you are looking. There are of course the standards—lethargy, a refusal for food, and quickly diminishing body weight, but often we are not aware that our Milk Snakes are under extreme stress until these signs begin showing, and then it may be too late.

What a keeper must do is discover the source of the stress and stamp it out. If the animal has a cagemate that it seems to avoid, separate the two of them. If there is no hidebox, or one that is not completely darkened or completely secure, you need to provide one that is. If the animal does not respond well to the sight of humans, cover the front of the tank. The point is, the only way to battle stress is find out its origins and eliminate them.

Mouth Rot/Infectious Stomatitis

Mouth rot is one of the most common physical diseases that attacks captive snakes. The bad news is, mouth rot can easily be fatal. The causes are multiple, but one of the more common ones is a lack of vitamin C (avitaminosis). The signs are somewhat pronounced, even if you are not looking for them—the snake will have trouble closing its mouth, the tissue around the gums and lining the mouth will appear pale and swollen, and, in the later stages of the disease's development, the snake's teeth will loosen and may actually fall out. Needless to say, the animal will not take any food during this time and will sit motionless in its cage (although some snakes will dip their heads in their waterbowl in an attempt to lessen the pain). If the

problem is allowed to get too far out of hand, the infection will spread down the windpipe, into the stomach, and the snake will eventually die.

However, treatment is not all that difficult. What the keeper must do is swab the infected areas with either a 3 % solution of hydrogen peroxide or a slightly diluted solution of the mouthwash called "Listerine." Both of these approaches have proved effective over the years and are thus recommended. The treatment should be performed at least twice a day for about five days, then once a day for the next two or three (unless of course the case was not that severe to begin with and the animal recovers more quickly). Beyond that, the keeper should up the snake's vitamin C intake by adding it in powdered form to its meals, in its drinking water, or by force-feeding.

External Parasitic Invasions (Mites and Ticks)

Another very common ailment of captive Milk Snakes, mites and ticks seem to spring up from nowhere. One of the common origins is the inclusion of one or both of these problems on a new specimen. Example—a keeper has ten tanks in his or her snake room, and the animals in each tank seem uninfested. Then a new snake is purchased at a show, pet store, etc., brought into the room, and suddenly, a month later, every animal has a group of tiny mites or a tick or two on them.

That is perhaps the most frequent cause of these two problems, but the causes aren't really the issue (the way to prevent it is by quarantining each new animal you receive for at least two weeks, checking it every day for any signs of this problem). The real question here is how to get rid of them once you've got them? We'll tackle each problem separately.

Ticks are tiny, teardrop-shaped creatures that attach themselves to any of the softer parts of a snake's body (under the scales) and feed off the animal's blood. Unlike mites, ticks don't appear in large quantities but instead in groups that only number up to a dozen (finding any more than that is unusual and means you've really got a red-alert case on your hands). The problem with ticks is that not only are they great for carrying and transmitting further disease organisms, but they are very hard to detect unless you're looking for them (which is why you should perform thorough "mite and tick checks" with a magnifying glass at least once a month). Once a tick is located, it seems a natural instinct to simply pinch it with your thumb and forefinger and just pull it right off. This is the wrong approach. It should be pointed out that ticks have an amazingly strong grip and if they are yanked in this manner there is a very real possibility that their heads will break off and remain in the snake's skin. If that happens, the keeper will then have further problems.

The correct approach is to grab the parasite as close to the snake's skin as possible with a pair of fine tweezers. Grip the tick firmly, but not hard enough to crush it, and pull slowly. If this technique does not work (because the tick is still strongly adherent), a second concept involves

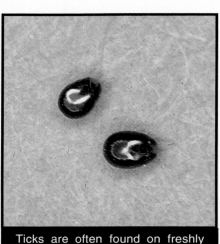

MICHAEL GILROY

Ticks are often found on freshly caught Milk Snake specimens. All new specimens should be inspected for ectoparasites before being included with the rest of your collection.

covering the tick with vaseline, cutting off its oxygen. In turn, the tick should release its grip or, in the very least, loosen it. If this also fails, you can always utilize the old classic "light a match, blow it out, and immediately apply it to the parasite" technique.

After you have removed the tick, swab the infected area with peroxide and spend a few further moments carefully inspecting the patient for other ticks.

Mites, on the other hand, can often be a lot more difficult to deal with. Not only will they exist in large colonies, they will also infest the snake's cage, the other snakes it will be housed with, and sometimes, in extreme cases, snakes in other cages and even the room they are all in. Having this happen in your attic or your cellar makes this prospect ugly enough, but imagine mites crawling all through the carpet or on the walls of your bedroom, living room, or den.

Again, the first thing you have to do is locate the problem. Although mites are very small, they can still be seen clearly with a magnifying glass. They appear as tiny brown dots moving about on the snake's body. They are most active at night, so perhaps you will want to check for them during these hours. In cases of extreme infestation, the feces of the mites can be seen as a silvery powder. Holding a snake toward a light source in just a certain way will reveal this. Another way of detecting mites, if you think you can stand it, is to simply hold the suspected snake in your hands for a few moments with white gloves on. Mites rarely miss the opportunity to jump on anything, and if the snake you're holding is infested, you'll know it.

The first step to eliminating them is to accurately judge how far the problem has gotten out of hand. Take all the snakes that are infested and quarantine them in their own group cage. Then take a small piece of pest strip (about a two-inch square will do) and wrap it in fine mesh screening. Staple the loose ends of the screening to a small block of wood, place the block into the infested snakes's tank, and leave it there for about a week. The reason for the screening is kind of obvious— pest strip is toxic to snakes and they should not be allowed to make direct contact with it (another way to conceal the strip is to place it in a small container with tiny holes drilled all through it). A waterbowl should not be included in the quarantine tank except during times when you or

Lampropeltis triangulum triangulum (Eastern Milk Snake). A Milk Snake's head is usually the best place to check for early signs of disease, most particularly around the eyes, mouth, and nostrils.

someone else reliable can supervise. Pest strip will infect a water source, so simply offer the water, watch the snakes drink it, then remove it. After the week is up, remove the strip and wait five to seven days, then place it in with them again so to kill of any newly hatched mites.

Finally, it goes without saying that the moment the infested snakes are diagnosed and removed from their normal tanks, the tank itself and all its contents should be either washed thoroughly in warm water and bleach (then rinsed in very cold) or disposed of.

Swellings and Blisters

Every now and then you may see soft swellings or whitish blisters on the surface of a Milk Snake' skin. The reasons these appear are many, but the way to "cure" them is relatively simple. As long as the swellings in question are not near an area of the animal that a keeper should definitely not be fooling with (like around the eyes, for example), he or she can simply make an incision in the infected area with a very sharp,

JOHN DOMMERS

Ideally, a Milk Snake's shed should come off in one whole piece, or, at the very least, only a few large pieces.

sterilized knife, drain any fluids therein, and swab the ensuing wound with peroxide or similar. This treatment should be given twice a day for the next week until the opening has closed and diversion of infection is assured.

It should be mentioned here that often times a blister or swelling will continually return, or more will appear in a very short time, in which case the problem will require greater treatment than the simple one outlined above. In such instances it is best to simply let a qualified veterinarian handle things, especially where the oral and optical regions are concerned.

Dysecdysis (Bad Shedding)

One of the more commonly encountered problems is trouble with shedding. Often times a snake will get through its normal shedding cycle—stop feeding, turn dull, eyes become cloudy then clear up—but then then skin does not come off in its ideal fashion, which is in one smooth, sock-like parcel. In cases like this the condition can be treated by simply soaking the snake in a bowl of warm water for a few minutes then trying to

removing the remaining shed yourself.

The area of the snake that you should be most concerned with is the eyes. If you have a Milk Snake that seems to be having trouble removing a brille (eye cap), you may have a serious problem. Not only can a strongly adherent eye cap infect the eye itself, it is possible for a snake to actually lose its vision altogether.

The first course of action is a simple one, using the warm water technique mentioned above. If that proves useless, try smearing the eye with mineral oil. Let the oil soak into the dried eye cap for about ten minutes, then try peeling the cap with tweezers or a thumb or fingernail. If the cap still refuses to come free, you will very likely have to bring the snake to a vet. The eyes of a snake are very delicate and should not be fooled with by amateurs. The approaches illustrated above are simple and thus for simple circumstances. If you feel the problem is out of your league, let a professional handle it. A snake will fall into a state of extreme stress and lethargy if it loses even a small part of its vision, and then you will end up with a dead pet.

TWO MORE "MILK SNAKES"

LAMPROPELTIS PYROMELANA AND *LAMPROPELTIS ZONATA*

As I discussed this book with a valued colleague of mine, Jerry G. Walls (who you may recognize as the co-author of the superb *Rat Snakes, A Hobbyist's Guide to Elaphe and Kin*), a most alarming conclusion came to light—between this and and its companion volume on kingsnakes, two of the eight *Lampropeltis* species were not covered whatsoever: the Sonoran Mountain Kingsnake, *Lampropeltis pyromelana*, and the somewhat less imaginatively named Mountain Kingsnake, *Lampropeltis zonata* (sometimes called the California Mountain Kingsnake although this name really isn't practical for a number of reason which I am not going to get into here). Knowing how very badly I wanted both of these books to paint a complete picture, I decided the only thing to do was bite the bullet and write an addendum covering the aforementioned species, their subspecies, and some other information as well.

THE SPECIES AND SUBSPECIES

I realize many of you are shaking your heads and saying, "Now wait a minute here. How come you're covering two 'king' snakes in a Milk Snake book?!" My answer to that is simple—because there is loads of evidence to suggest that these two species are much more closely related to *Lampropeltis triangulum* (Milk Snakes) than to *Lampropeltis getula* (Common Kingsnakes). Common names can be very misleading, as you now are doubtless aware. I will still refer to the snakes in this chapter as kingsnakes simply because most of

you know them as such, but in light of the true relational factors that tie animals together in that wacky web of nebulous knowledge called taxonomy, both of these species are really Milk Snakes and not kings at all.

Let's start with the snakes themselves and give a little discussion of each.

Sonoran Mountain Kingsnake
Lampropeltis pyromelana
(Cope, 1886)

Perhaps the more commercially successful of the two mountain kingsnake species, this pretty snake grows to about 41 in/104 cm and boasts the typical red/black/white color scheme of the tri-colored *Lampropeltis* snakes. The snout is usually white, black with white flecking, or pale yellow. The thickness of the banding (of all three colors) varies tremendously, some colors being completely obscured in

DON SODERBERG

Lampropeltis pyromelana infralabialis (Utah Mountain Kingsnake).

certain specimens. The scales are smooth and number between 23 and 25 at midbody and the anal plate is undivided. General range of this species is Utah, Nevada, Arizona, and into northern Mexico.

Utah Mountain Kingsnake
Lampropeltis pyromelana infralabialis
Tanner, 1953

A standout feature of this subspecies is the fact that it has only nine infralabials whereas the others have ten. A resident of Arizona, Nevada, and, of course, Utah, it has a white snout that stands out from the rest of the head, which is black. Adults can grow as long as 40 in/102 cm. This snake is

R. G. MARKEL

Lampropeltis pyromelana knoblochi (Chihuahua Mountain Kingsnake).

aware there aren't any specimens for sale. (Don't quote me on that, however.) This snake grows to about 42 in/102 cm although the average is more like 36 in/91 cm. It is nocturnal and apparently very cryptic. It feeds largely on lizards and mice, the latter of which seem to be taken without fuss by captive adults.

Arizona Mountain Kingsnake
Lampropeltis pyromelana pyromelana
(Cope, 1886)

Probably the subspecies most commonly seen in the hobby, the Arizona Mountain Kingsnake has been bred through many generations and can still command a respectable price. In many ways their popularity is difficult to understand. The young can be very difficult to feed (most of them will only want very tiny lizards) and the adult females usually have very small egg clutches (maybe four or five at best).

Found in Chihuahua and Sonora in Mexico and then north through central Arizona, this snake can grow up to 42 in/107 cm and will have

only rarely seen in the hobby and is usually very expensive.

Chihuahua Mountain Kingsnake
Lampropeltis pyromelana knoblochi
Taylor, 1940

A resident of northern Mexico, very little was known about this snake's natural history until a few specimens found their way into the herpetocultural hobby. Now they are being bred in captivity (not regularly, though, since there still aren't that many around) and even a beautiful albino form has surfaced although as far as I am

LOUIS PORRAS

Lampropeltis pyromelana pyromelana (Arizona Mountain Kingsnake).

over 40 narrow white rings encircling its body. The head is mostly black, but the snout is usually white or pale yellow with dark mottling.

Huachuca Mountain Kingsnake
Lampropeltis pyromelana woodini

Lampropeltis pyromelana woodini (Huachuca Mountain Kingsnake). Neonatal specimen.

Tanner, 1953

Although very similar to *L. p. pyromelana*, *woodini* can be distinguished from its sister subspecies by a lower body ring count—this snake usually has less than 40, whereas *pyromelana* will have more. It is found exclusively in the Huachuca Mountains in southern Arizona and Mexico and has a white snout tipping a uniformly black head. It grows to about 44 in/112 cm. Rarely seen in the hobby, captives reportedly do fairly well, feeding on lizards and small rodents which they seem to take without too much provocation on the part of the keeper.

Mountain Kingsnake
Lampropeltis zonata
(Lockington, 1876)

Sometimes referred to as the California Mountain Kingsnake, *L. zonata* is one of the most beautiful serpents in all of North America.

General range of the species includes southwestern Oregon, California (largely along the coast), and into Baja, but there is also a tiny disjunct population in southern Washington along (and just crossing over) the Oregon border. The coloring is again, as with *L. pyromelana*, typical of the tri-colored Milk Snakes—red/black/and white (although in some examples the red is absent), being situated as rings that occasionally cross over the belly, depending on the specimen. The snout is usually uniform black but can be speckled with red, but white snouts are unknown.

San Pedro Mountain Kingsnake
Lampropeltis zonata agalmae
Van Denburgh and Slevin, 1923

Rarely growing over 30 in/76 cm, the San Pedro Mountain Kingsnake is native to the northern sector of Baja California and the Sierra Jarez and Sierra San Pedro Martir, Mexico. It is a very "bright" snake because it has a great amount of red as compared to others of the species (some of which are represented by

Lampropeltis zonata agalmae (San Pedro Mountain Kingsnake).

specimens that have no red at all). This particular snake is virtually

Lampropeltis zonata **(Mountain Kingsnake)**, by A. v. d. Neuwenhuizen.

JOHN R. QUINN

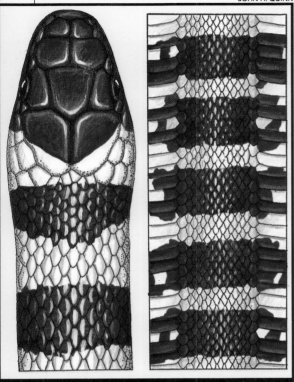

Lampropeltis zonata herrerae (Todos Santos Island Kingsnake).

are around 7 in/18 cm at hatching.

Sierra Mountain Kingsnake
Lampropeltis zonata multicincta
(Yarrow, 1882)

This snake intergrades with the St. Helena Mountain Kingsnake where their ranges overlap, most predominantly in southwestern Oregon. Occurring primarily in the Sierra Nevadas from Kern and Tulare Counties to Shasta County in central and northern California, the Sierra Mountain Kingsnake is found most often in wooded sections of canyons. It is a hardy snake that feeds on lizards, rodents, and occasionally small birds, but is virtually never seen in the hobby because the state it is endemic to is very protective of its herpetofauna.

Coastal Mountain Kingsnake
Lampropeltis zonata multifasciata
(Bocourt, 1886)

Another of the "redder" Mountain Kings, *multifasciata* even has a bit of this lovely color on the snout. There are usually less than 41 black-white-black triads on the body, each being about the same in width as the red rings that separate them.

never seen in the hobby but reportedly does well in captivity.

Todos Santos Island Kingsnake
Lampropeltis zonata herrerae
Van Denburgh and Slevin, 1923

This is one of the Mountain Kings that lacks red coloration to the degree where it could be mistaken at a distance for a ringed California Kingsnake, *Lampropeltis getula californiae*. It is virtually unknown to both hobbyists and professional herpetologists alike, but it can be assumed that much of its natural history is similar to that of the other Mountain King forms, i.e., it probably eats mice and lizards without hesitation, has small egg clutches, etc. Adults grow to about 30 in/76 cm on average and the young, which resemble the adults,

Lampropeltis zonata multicincta (Sierra Mountain Kingsnake).

WILLIAM B. ALLEN, JR.

Lampropeltis zonata (Mountain Kingsnake), by B. Kahl.

R. T. ZAPPALORTI

Lampropeltis zonata multifasciata (Coastal Mountain Kingsnake).

Like the Sierra Mountain Kingsnake, this one also favors wooded and shaded areas in and near canyons, often close to quiet streams. As its name suggests, it is native to areas very close to the coast, in select sections of central California. This is one snake not likely to be seen in the herpetocultural hobby.

San Bernardino Mountain Kingsnake

Lampropeltis zonata parvirubra
Zweifel, 1952

Now here's a snake with an interesting feeding behavior—

Lampropeltis zonata parvirubra (San Bernardino Mountain Kingsnake).

R. G. MARKEL

apparently, according to a 1976 report by Goodman and Goodman, specimens of *parvirubra* would lie in an open area in the hopes of encouraging attacks from nesting birds, then use these attacks to locate the birds's nests, of course taking the nestlings as food. Assuming these reports are indeed accurate, the evidence suggests that this species (or at the least, this subspecies) is fairly "intelligent." Growing to a length of about 40 in/ 102 cm, it can be found in southern California along foothills, moist to semi-moist woodlands, and in canyons and valleys. It is almost never seen in captivity.

San Diego Mountain Kingsnake

Lampropeltis zonata pulchra
Zweifel, 1952

The San Diego Mountain Kingsnake is one of two subspecies of Mountain King that is occasionally seen in the hobby (and, like the other, can be a real drain on the wallet). Native to a few counties in extreme southern California, the number of triads on the body can

DR. R. S. FUNK

Lampropeltis zonata pulchra (San Diego Mountain Kingsnake).

St. Helena Mountain Kingsnake
Lampropeltis zonata zonata
(Lockington, 1876)

A creature of woodland habitats, it is little-studied and thus poorly known. Never seen for sale commercially, it is known to take lizards, small mice, and small snakes. It does not grow over 40 in/ 102 cm and the black rings often touch along the median keel (meaning they are "confluent"). The snout and most of the head are uniformly black, the first white ring beginning at the posterior margin of the mouth. Juveniles are usually about 7 in/18 cm long and may appear "brighter" than the adults due to the brilliance of the white rings.

vary greatly—anywhere from 27 to 38, making identification somewhat difficult. It is a pretty good captive considering the reputation most Mountain Kings have, the adults taking mice (and small snakes and lizards) whereas the young, usually very fussy, will sometimes take small mice too. As far as keepability is concerned, this is probably the best subspecies. Some specimens are also stunning examples of how beautiful snakes can be.

KEEPING *L. PYROMELANA* AND *L. ZONATA* IN CAPTIVITY

If you have decided to go out and get yourself one of these beautiful little snakes and are sure you can provide it with the food items it requires, then I congratulate you on your impeccable taste in herps. I'll say one thing for these two species— they certainly are visually stunning. In fact, it is my opinion that the mountain kings, which I will collectively refer to both species as from here on, are the most striking members of the genus *Lampropeltis*. I realize my opinion isn't going to affect yours one way or another, but it's my book so what the heck.

Seriously, though, these are remarkably pretty animals and thus a natural sorrow for their occasionally uncooperative dispositions is also be present. There isn't a lot of information available for the precise husbandry of each subspecies (many, I suspect, haven't been kept at all, with the exception of a few zoo cases), but it is safe to assume the details are

Lampropeltis zonata zonata (St. Helena Mountain Kingsnake).

MIKE DEE

pretty much the same with one as it is for all. So, as I said in the last paragraph, if you've gone out and bought a mountain king you have my admiration. Now you have to know how to keep it alive.

SETTING UP THE TANK

Since most mountain kingsnakes are residents of fairly warm and fairly dry habitats, you can pretty much set them up in a basic snake tank—a 10-gallon tank (per adult specimen) with an inch or two of sterile potting soil, a few rocks, a hidebox, and a water bowl. According to some data I dug up here and there, plants are not necessary because they end up getting uprooted and lying around like fallen soldiers. You can, however, put in a sturdy branch or two. Other embellishments that will add to the tank's visual esthetics include some pine cones and pine needles, a few leaves, and maybe even some fallen tree bark (all of which has to be replaced when cleaning time comes around—keep that in mind). A generic equivalent to this setup (this is a concept I am going to start using a lot in my future writings) goes something like this—a plastic sweaterbox (tape the lid shut or use rubber bands) with some soft paper toweling as a substrate, a plastic water bowl with a wide base (so it won't tip) and a plastic shoebox with more paper toweling on the floor and a hole cut into the lid. One rock should be added so the snake can begin a shed on it, and one branch for climbing. Simple, easy to clean, and, in my opinion, the best setup of the two. I, in fact, would even emit the branch and make the cage totally artificial, with the exception of the rock, of course. Why? Because in an environment as "sterile" as this, you

Lampropeltis zonata (Mountain Kingsnake).

WILLIAM B. ALLEN, JR.

K. H. SWITAK

Lampropeltis zonata agalmae (San Pedro Mountain Kingsnake).

know darn well the snake is going to be as safe as it can be and thus live out a long life. That, I believe, is the main goal of a keeper, and I can say from experience that simple, clinical enclosures like this almost guarantee a snake's well-being. I'm almost embarrassed to tell you how long I've managed to keep some notoriously difficult species with this arrangement.

As for temperature, humidity, and all that other climatic stuff, a good ambient temperature is around 77 to 84°F (25 to 29°C) with a small drop of about three or four degrees at night is sufficient. Humidity can be kept moderate at best since these animals don't really need a great amount of moisture. Remember, they are for the most part woodland-dwellers. Also, don't be disappointed if you don't see your mountain kings much; they are for the most part nocturnal and even then quite secretive. They are very inquisitive creatures but don't seem to care for daylight much. Some varieties are active during the day in early summer when temperatures are fairly cool, but as a general rule most of them hunt during the dark hours, so be aware.

FEEDING MOUNTAIN KINGSNAKES

Four items—mice, lizards, birds, and small snakes. If your mountain king doesn't accept one of these in some form or another, then you've got problems. Rules for feeding, force-feeding, and so on can be found in the feeding chapter. That's all you need to know.

BREEDING MOUNTAIN KINGSNAKES

From the data I have gathered with the invaluable assistance of friend, colleague, and fellow keeper Erik D. Stoops from Arizona, it seems

Lampropeltis zonata multicincta (Sierra Mountain Kingsnake).

apparent that mountain kings really aren't all that difficult to breed; what seems to be the real challenge is feeding the neonates (not because they aren't willing but because of what they require). More on this in a moment.

The whole process begins with a cooling period that lasts about three or four months and involves an ambient temperature of about 63°F/ 17°C (a mild hibernation, if you will). Then the adults are removed and placed in a breeding tank, which can consist of a male and a female or, if you prefer, two males, who will possibly perform a combat ritual of sorts that could serve to stimulate them even further. Also, if the female is really in the mood, she will lift her tail and spray an attracting scent all about the cage. It is also important to remember that a mountain king's ambient temperature need not be higher than about 77°F/25°C. If it is too warm the ensuing eggs probably will be infertile.

After successful copulation comes a gestation period of about 60 days. Then, as egglaying time draws near, a keeper should provide a nesting box filled with moistened granular vermiculite or, if he or she wishes, a tank entirely bedded with the same. The reason for the thick substrate is so the female will have a place to burrow until she lays. The eggs are about a half an inch long, white, smooth, and oval, and number between four and five (although nine has been recorded). The eggs usually do not cluster but it is still good for the keeper to be around when they are laid just in case. The incubation box can also contain moistened vermiculite, or, sphagnum moss (or a combination of both).

Incubation time takes about 68 days and the young will measure about 5 to 8 inches. They will resemble their parents almost exactly and feed on tiny lizards (skinks and geckos are much-loved). This, as I said before, is often the major stumbling block because even if a keeper could supply these items, he or she probably wouldn't want to use them as food. However, it has been recorded mountain king babies that feed well on tiny lizards usually switch over to pinkie mice in a

LUDWIG TRUTNAU

Lampropeltis zonata multicincta (Sierra Mountain Kingsnake).

relatively short time (about three to six months), so there is still hope. Furthermore, virtually all neonates take not only live tiny lizards but frozen and thawed ones as well.

For more information, I can offer you two references that will be helpful. The first is an article by Ludwig Trutnau in the October, 1991 issue of *Tropical Fish Hobbyist* magazine on the breeding of *Lampropeltis zonata*. The other, by the same author, is a book called *Nonvenomous Snakes* that has some otherwise hard-to-find information on the breeding of *Lampropeltis pyromelana* (plus some more *zonata* info).

Lampropeltis zonata (Mountain Kingsnake).

WILLIAM B. ALLEN, JR

SUGGESTED READING

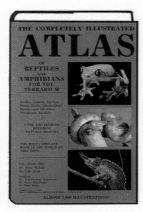

H-1102, 830 pgs, 1800+ photos

TS-165, 2 VOLUME SET 655 pgs, 1850+ photos

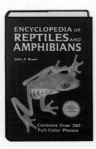

PS-207, 230 pgs, B&W Illus.

H-935, 576 pgs, 260+ photos

PS-876, 384 pgs, 175+ photos

KW-197, 128 pgs, 110+ photos

PB-126, 64 pgs, 32+ photos

AP-925, 160 pgs, 120+ photos

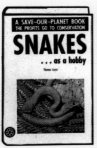

KW-197, 128 pgs, 110+ photos

J-007, 48 pgs, 25+ photos

TU-015, 64 pgs, 50+ photos

TW-111, 256 pgs, 180+ photos